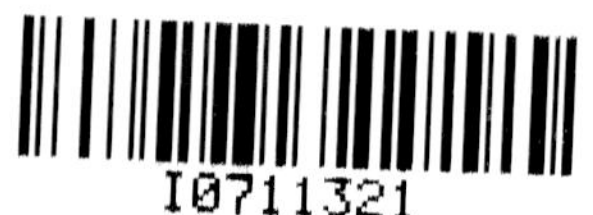

Hello Dear,
Thank you for your order,
Much appreciate your purchase from us.
Hope we can get positive feedback from
you ;)
Have a great day!

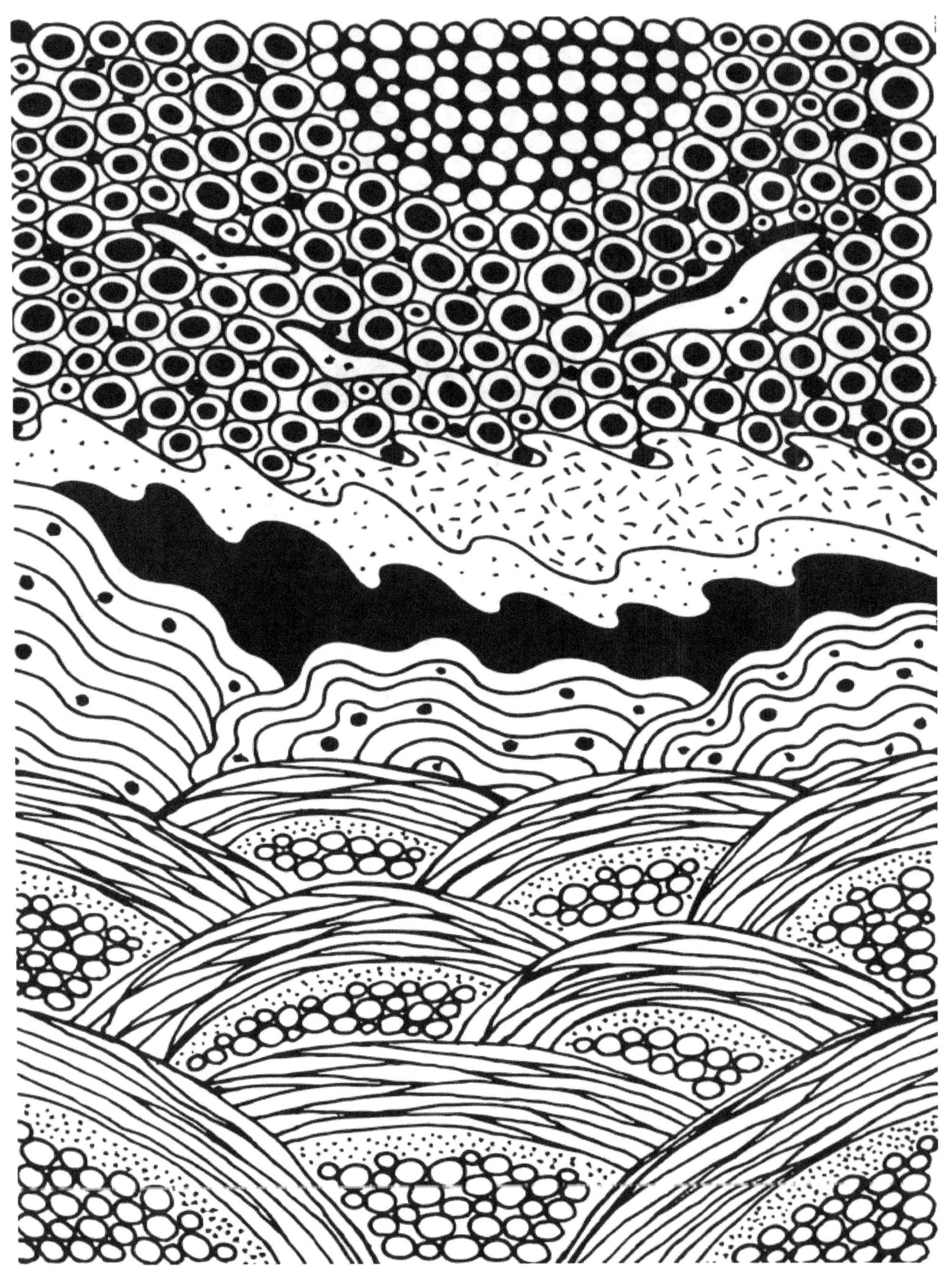

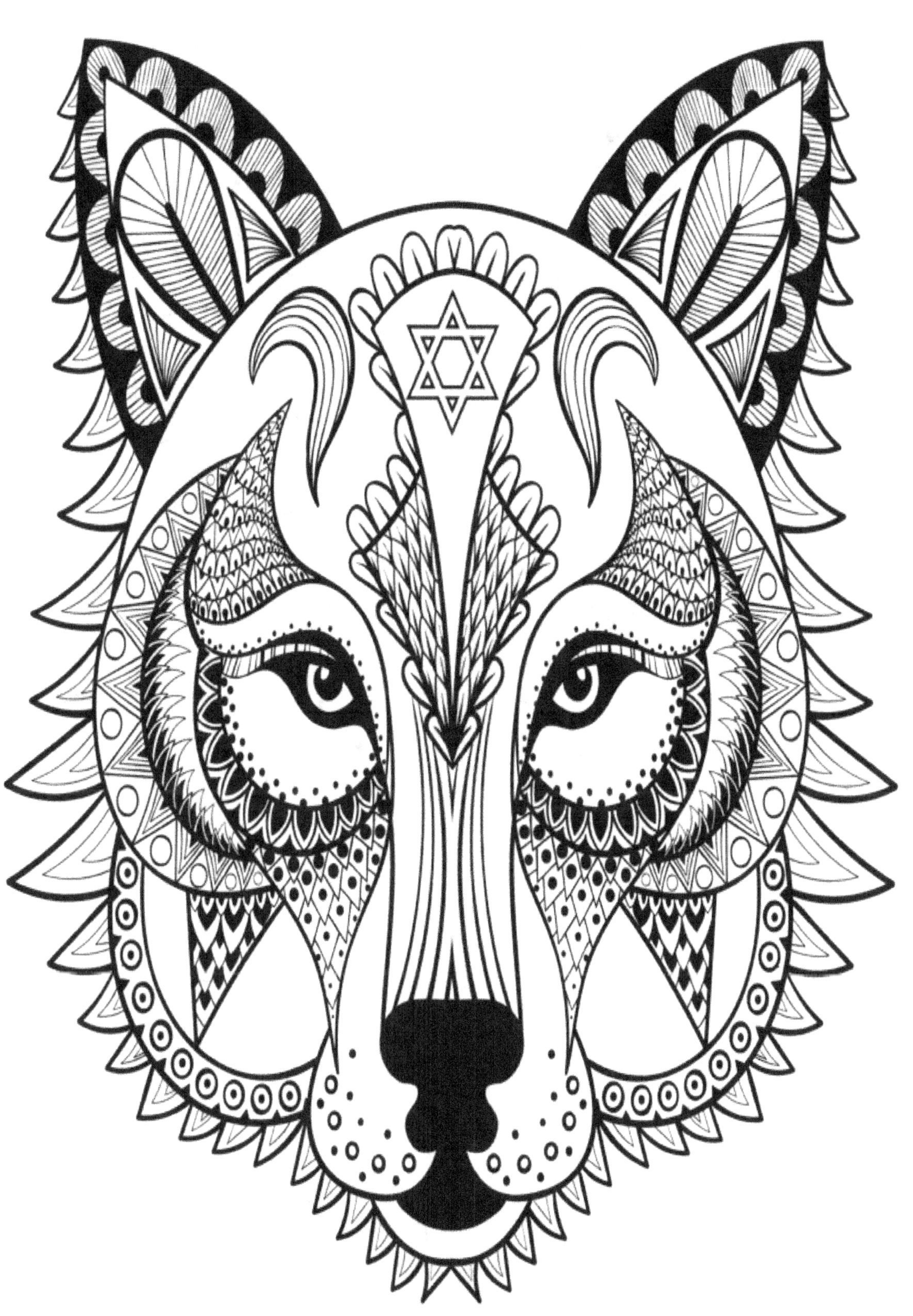

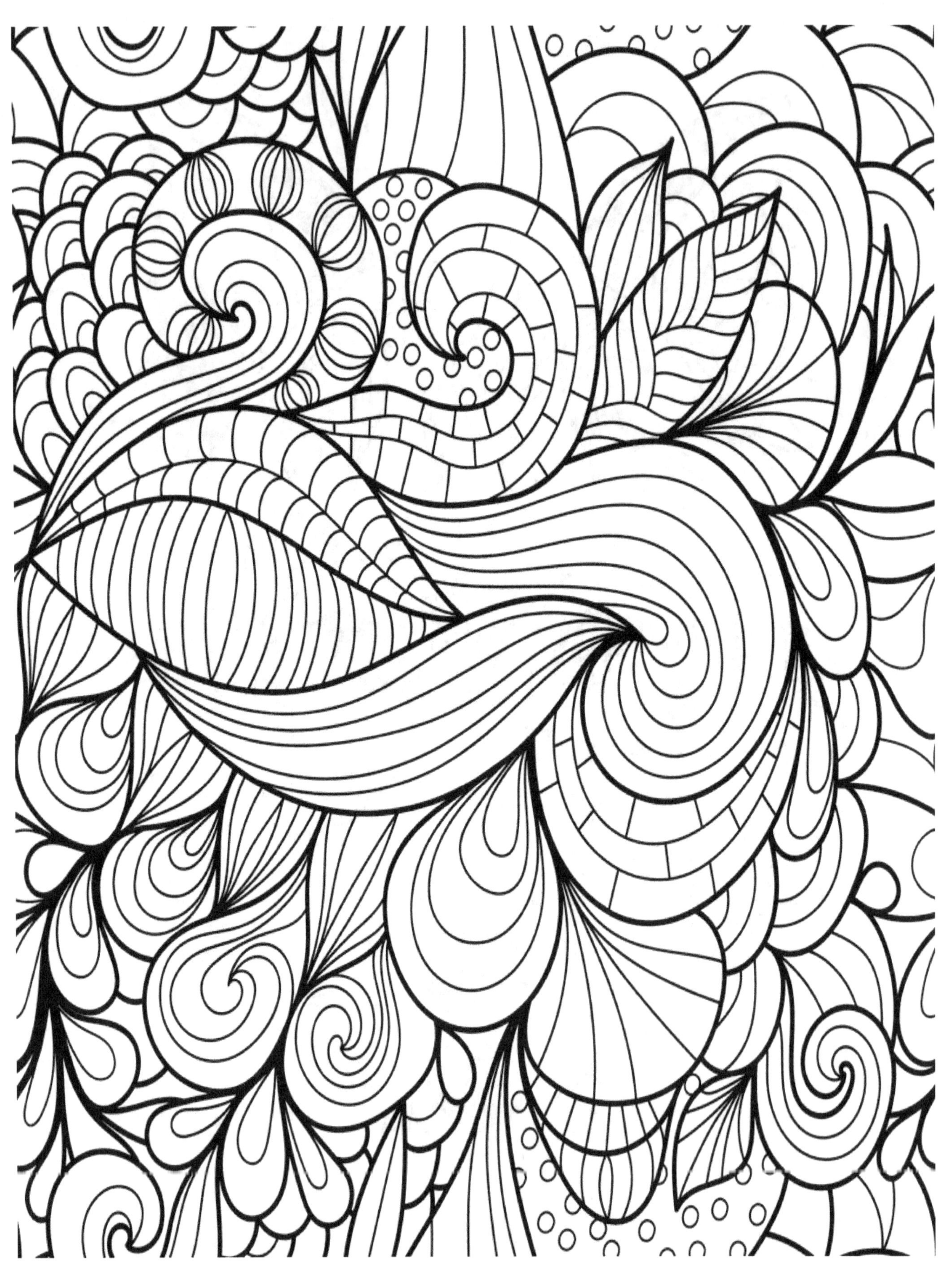

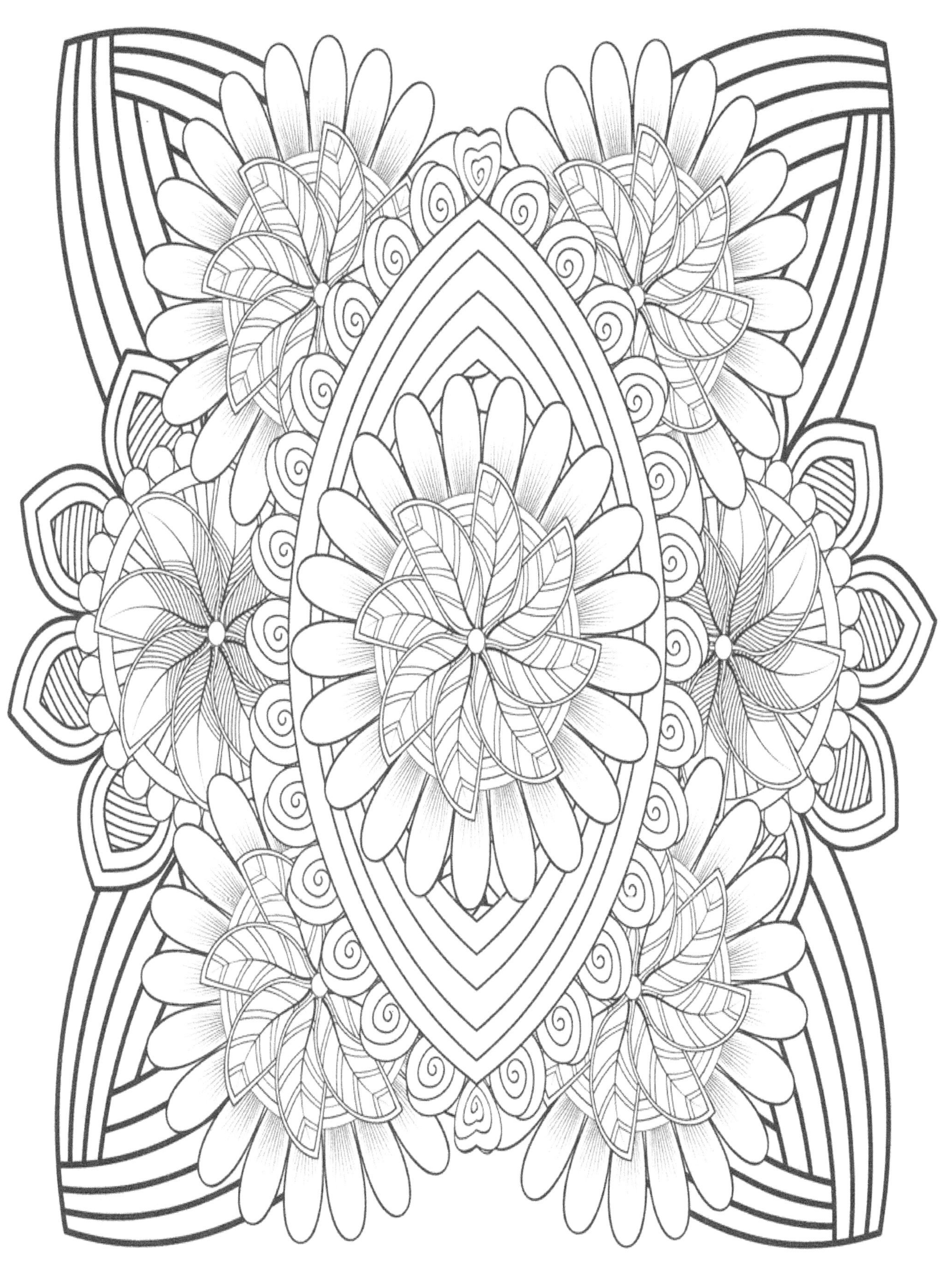

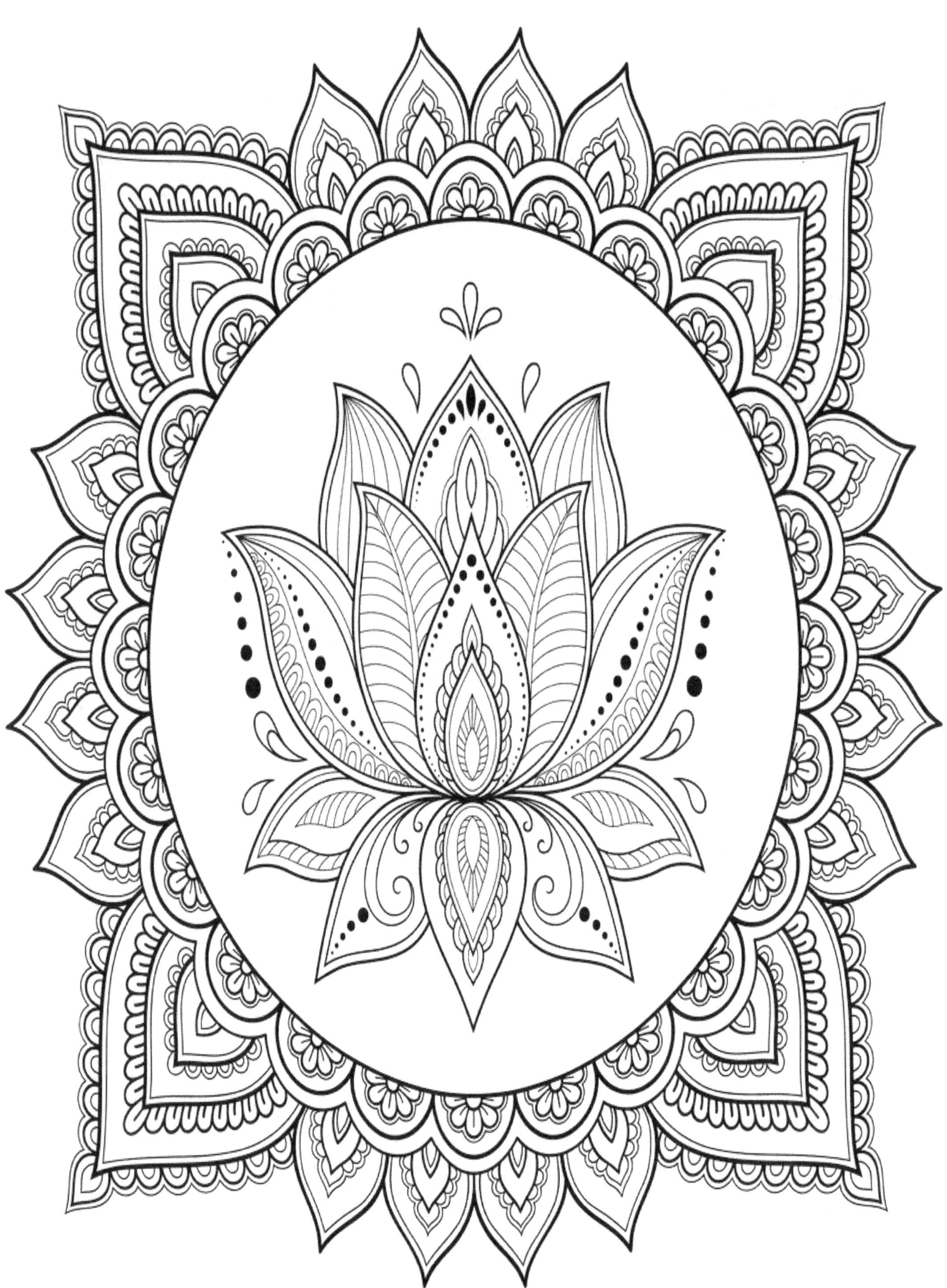

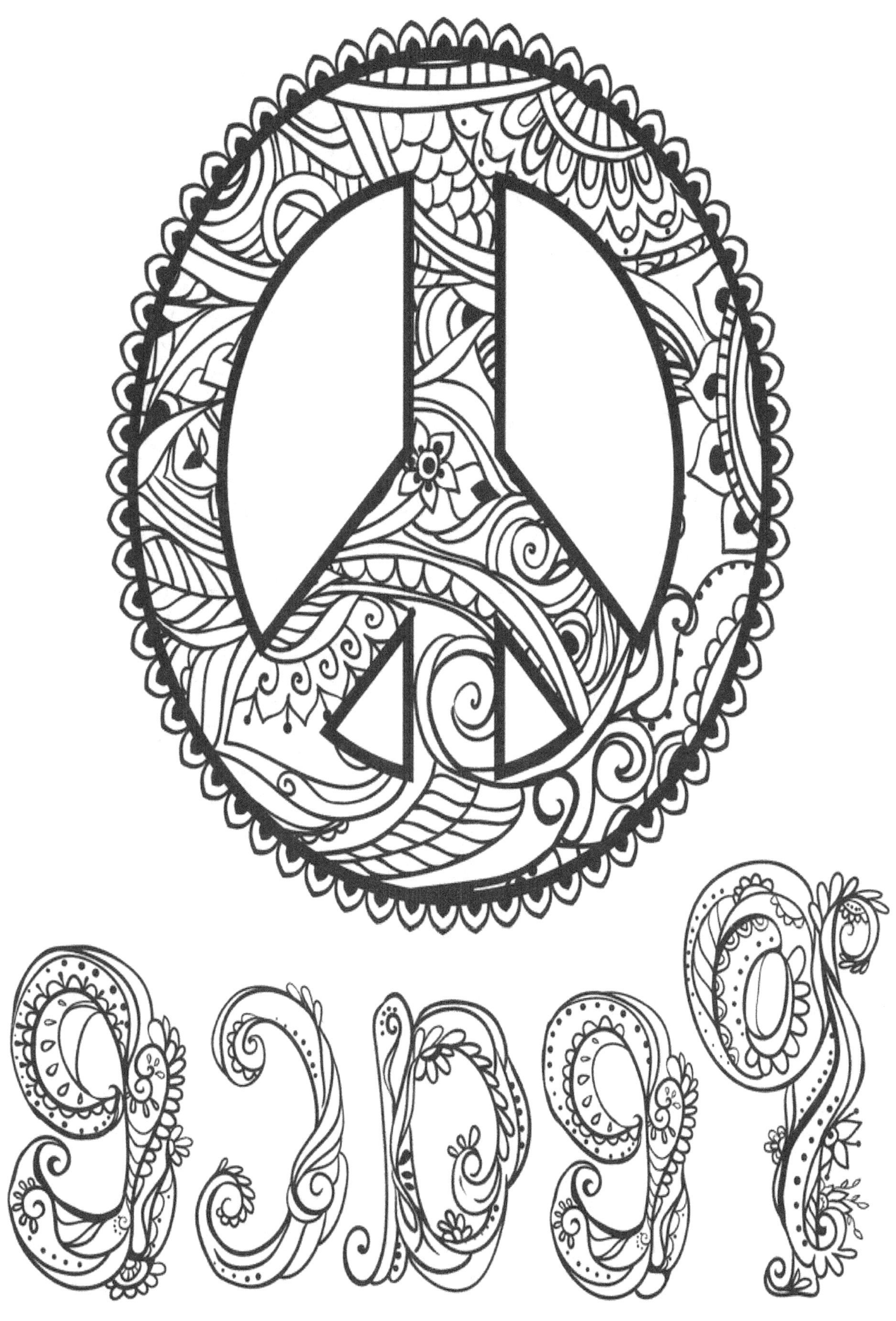

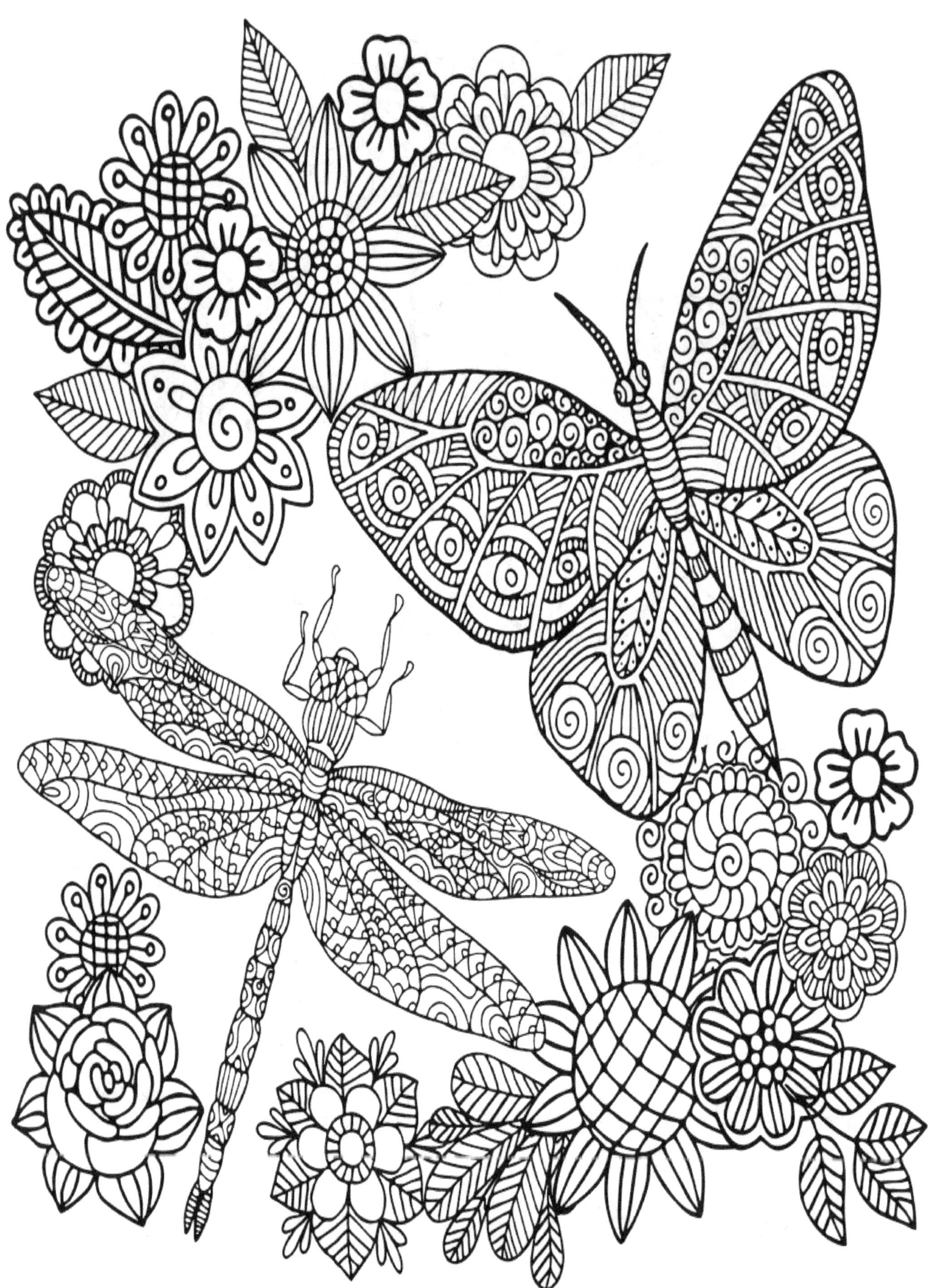

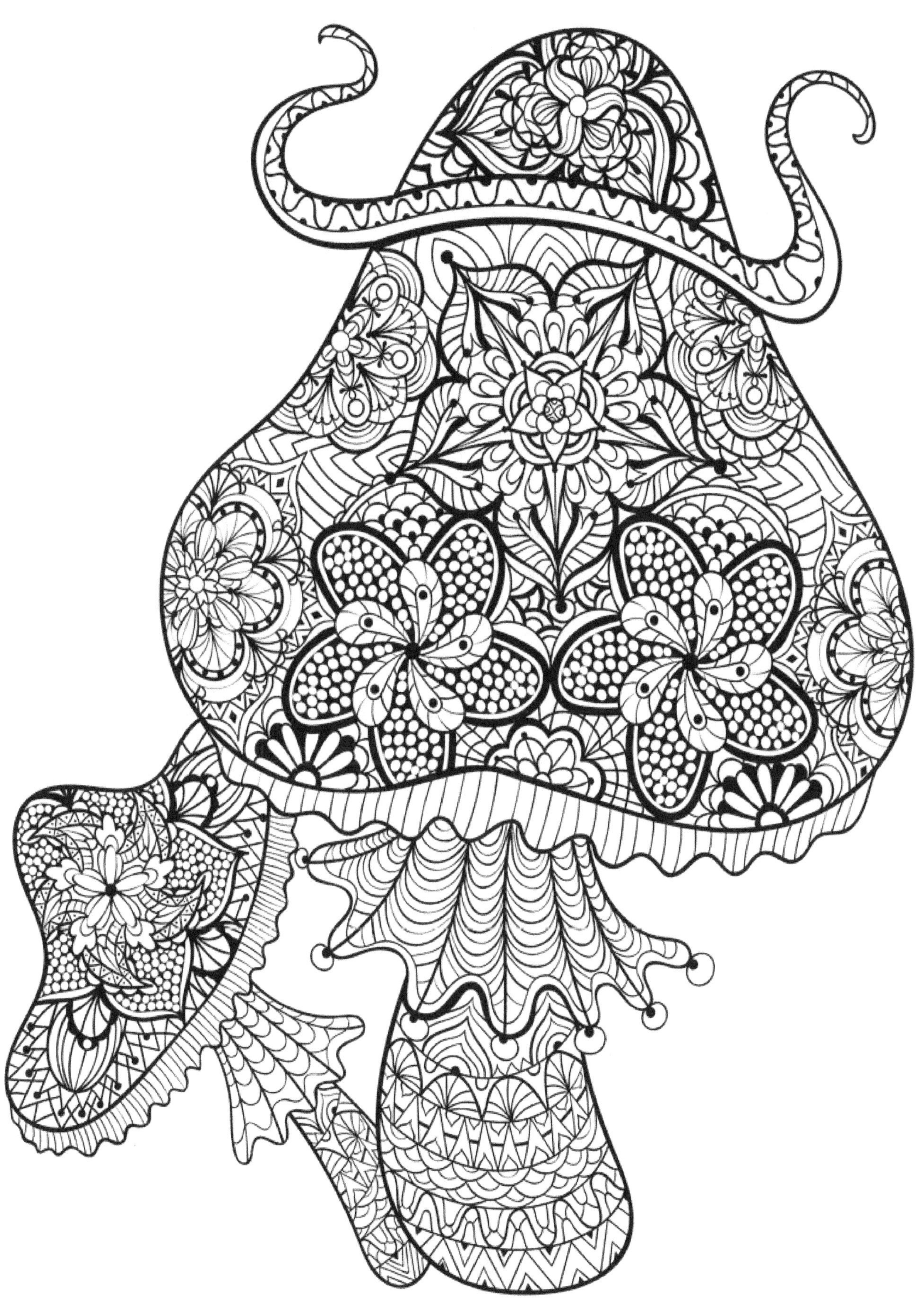

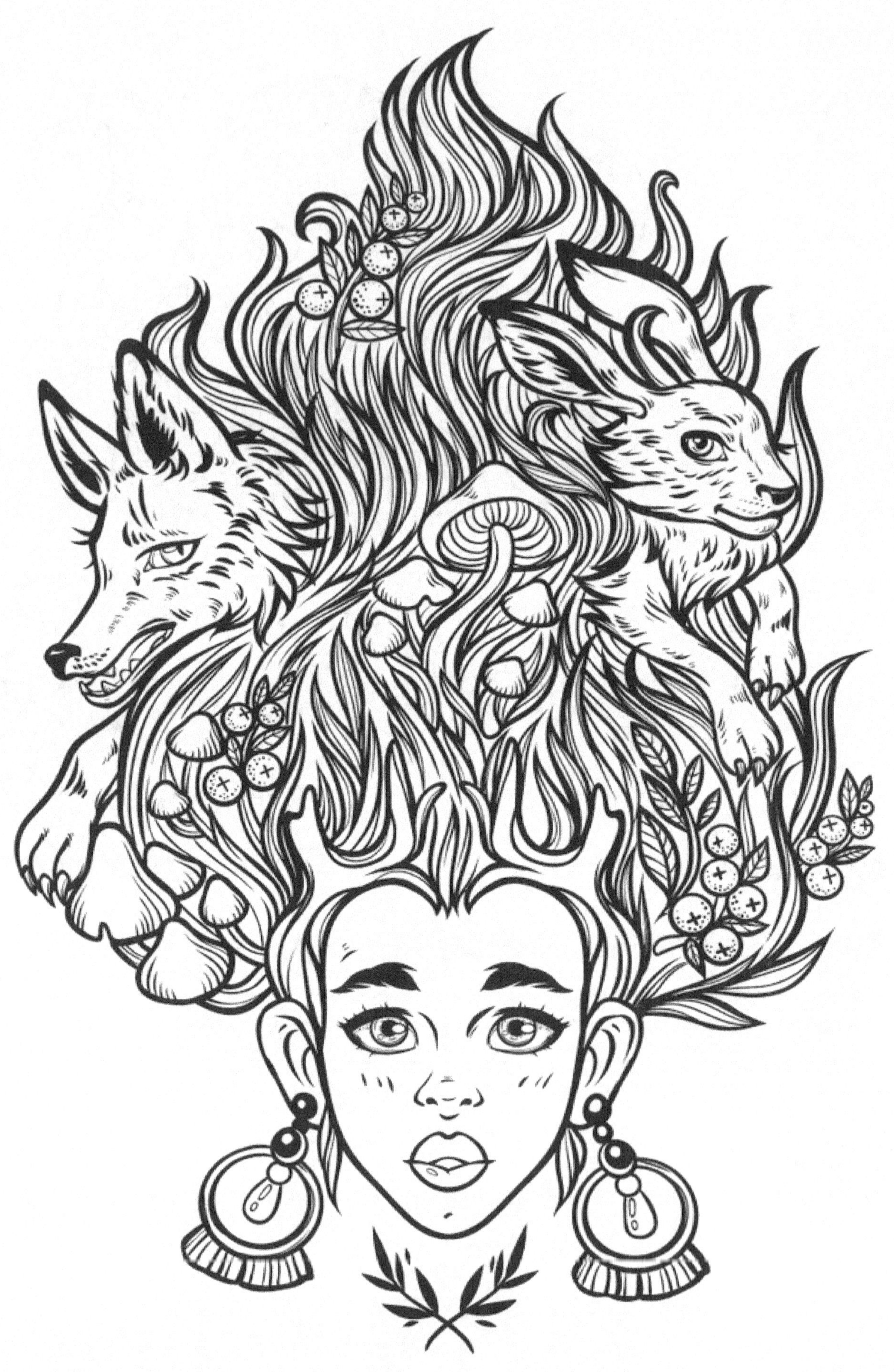

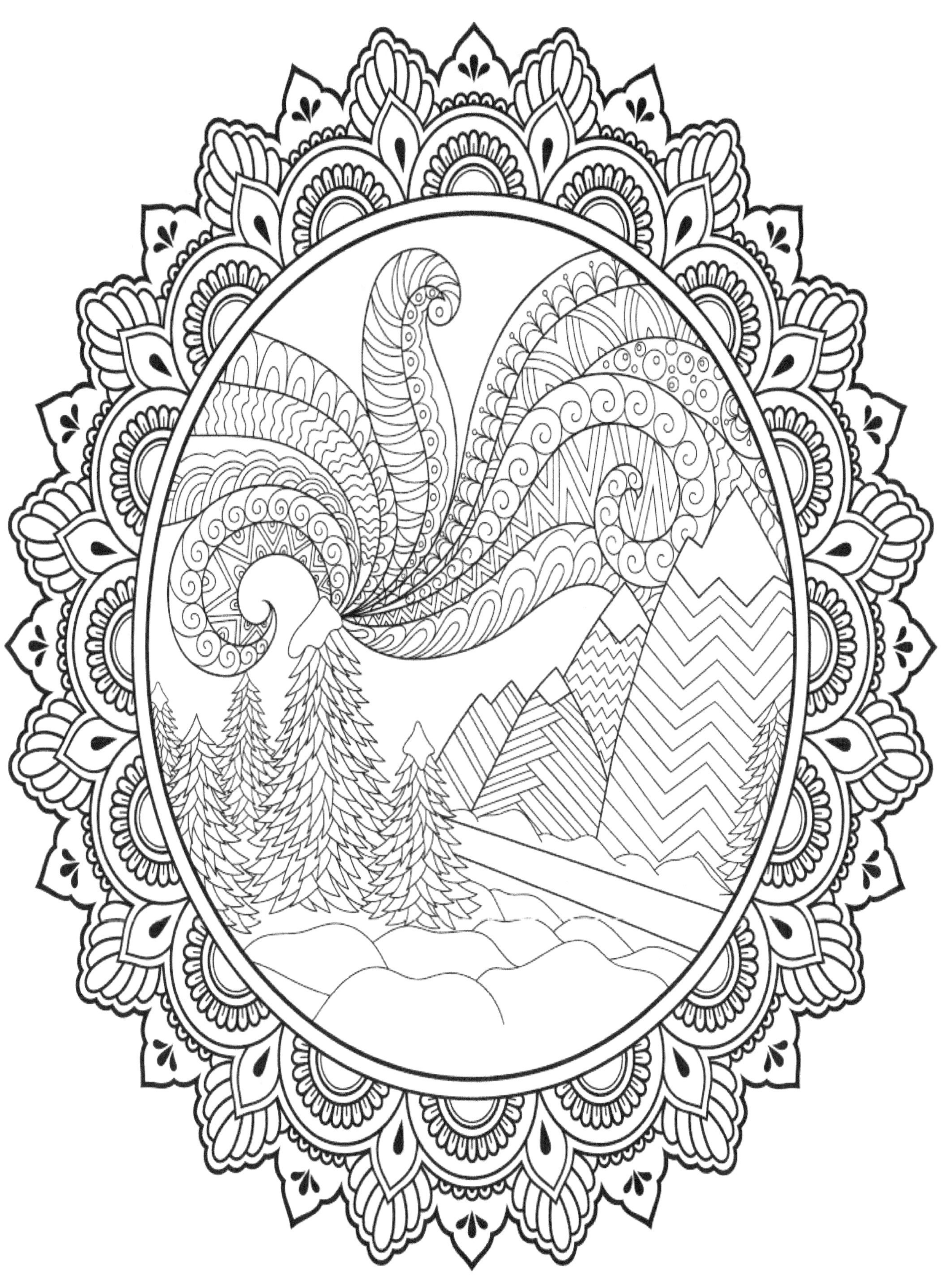

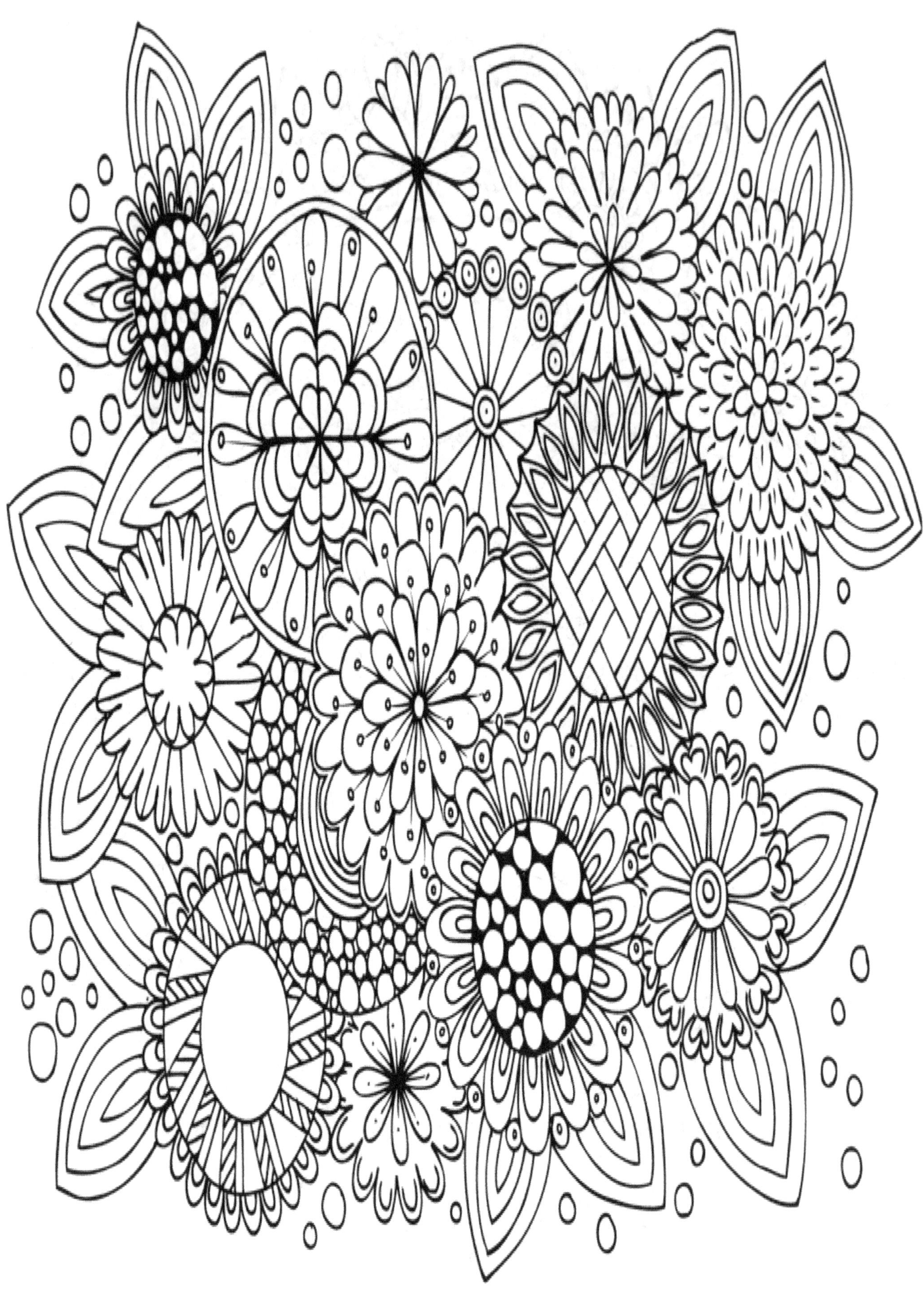

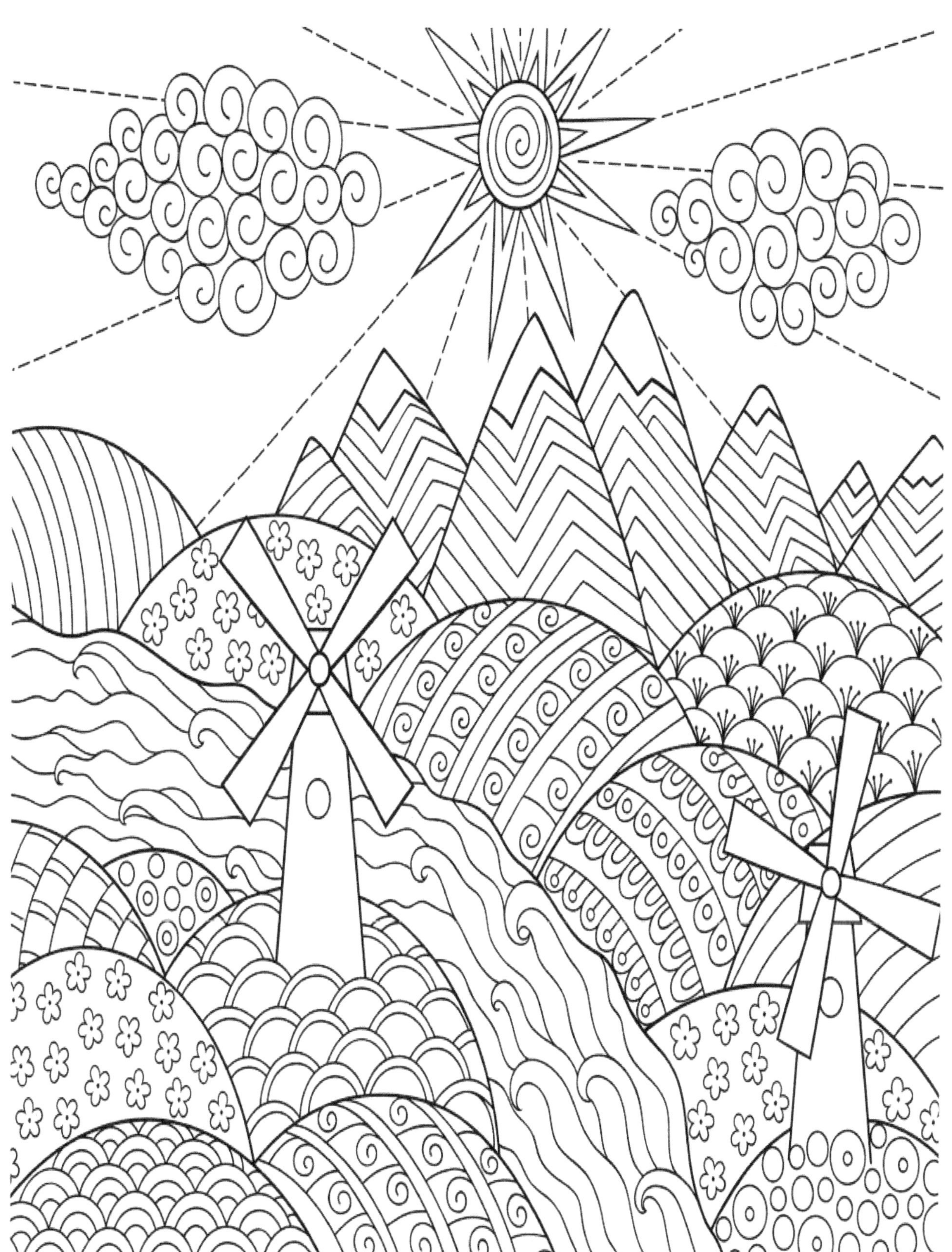

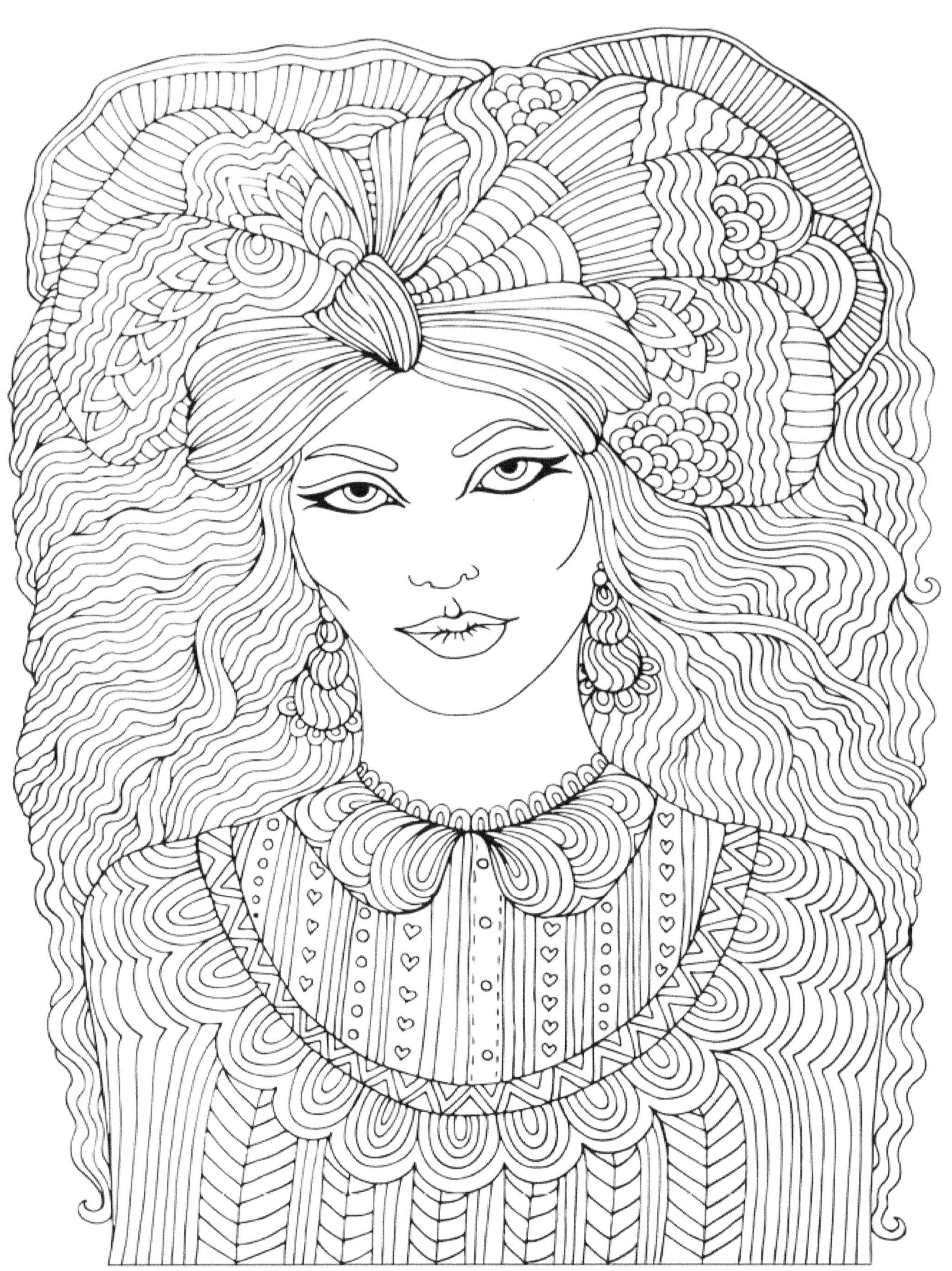

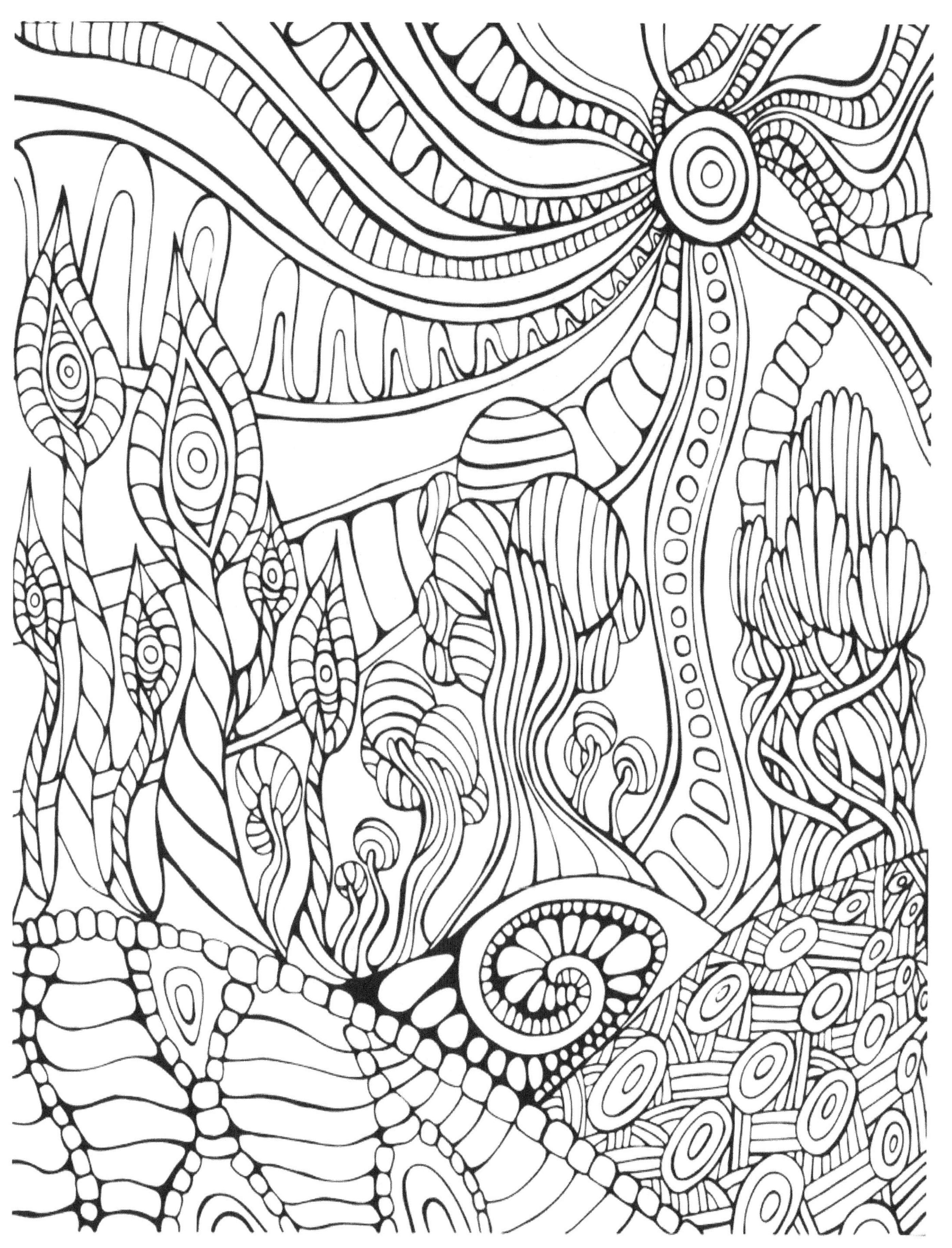

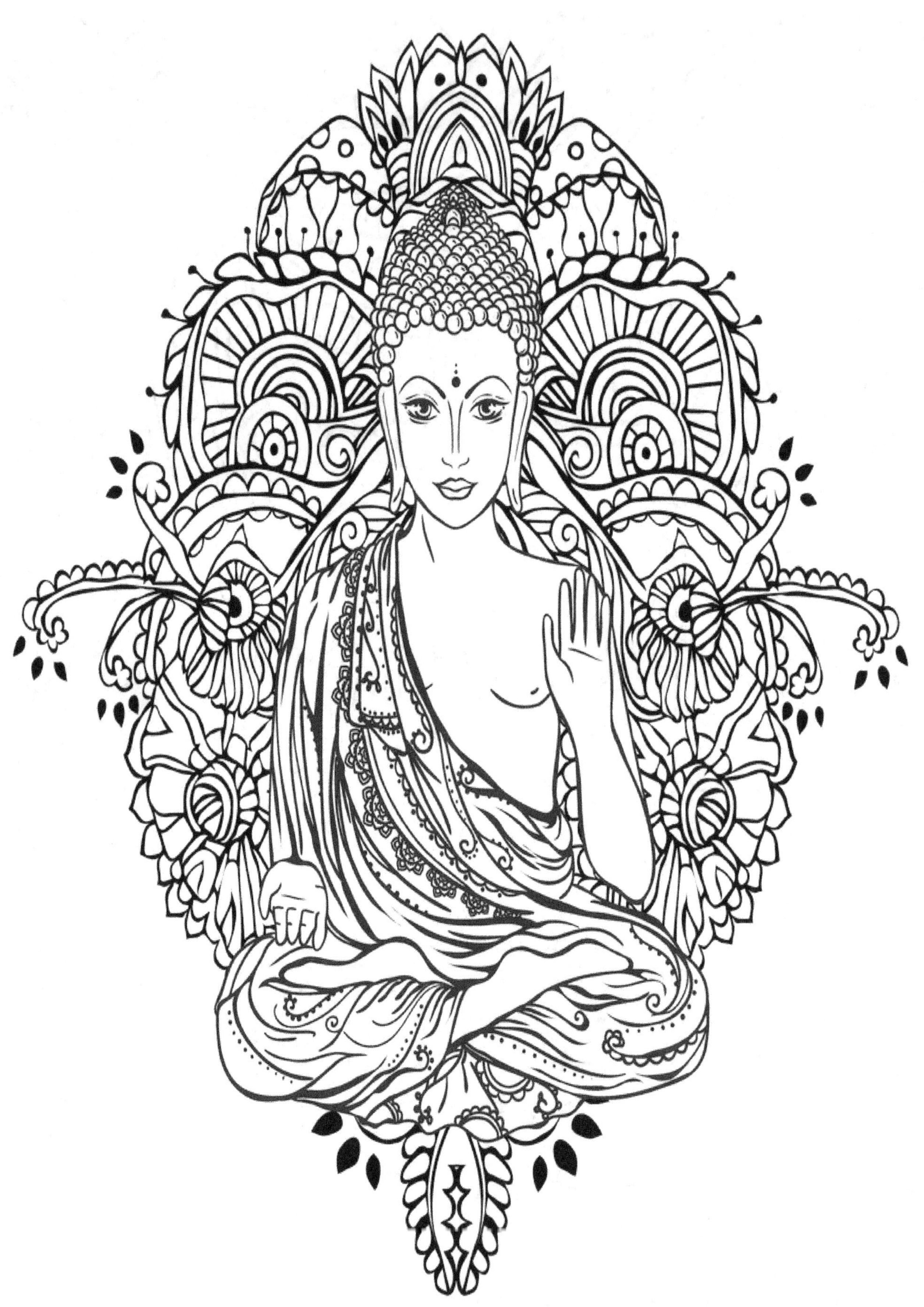

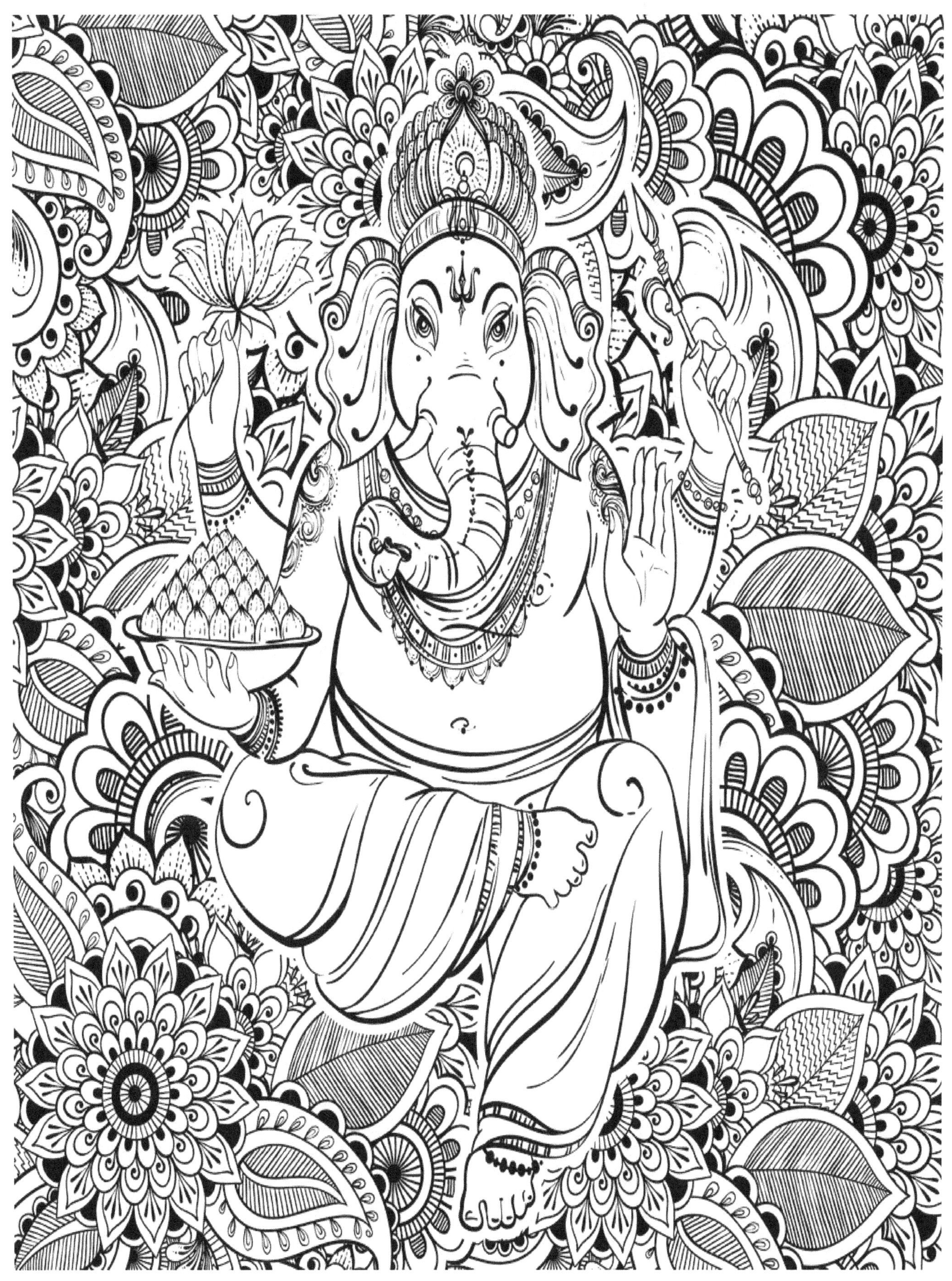

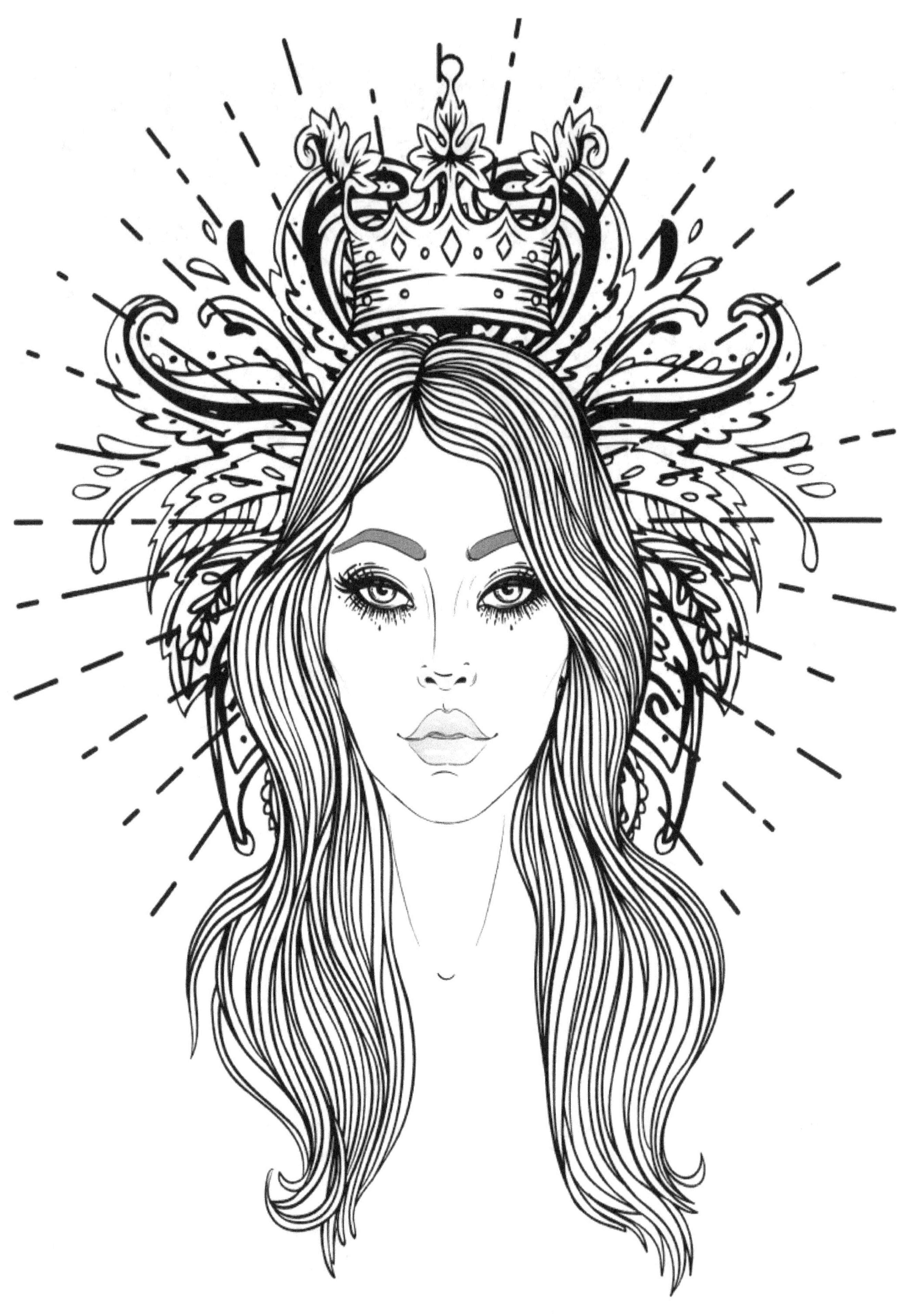

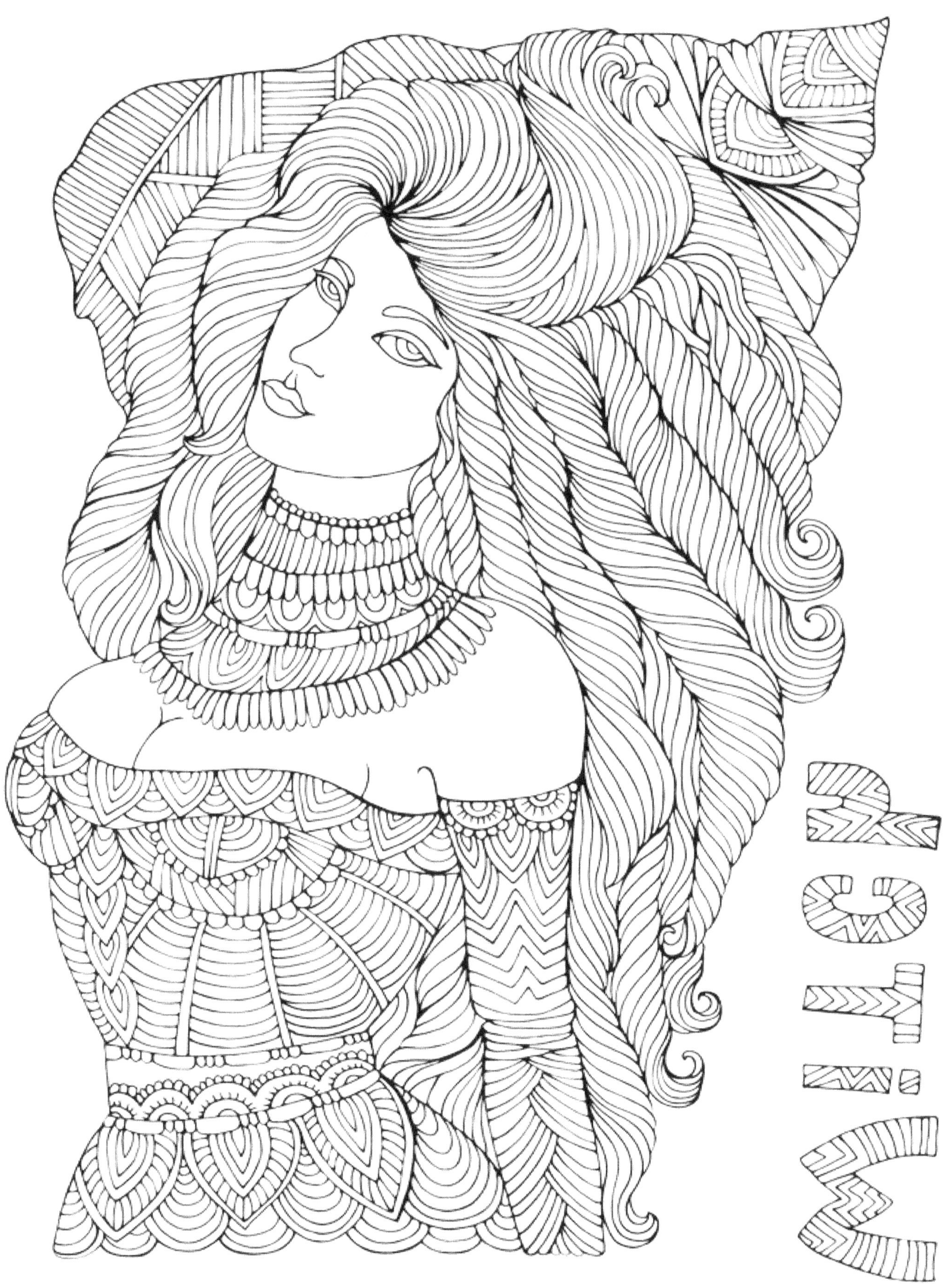
MAGIC

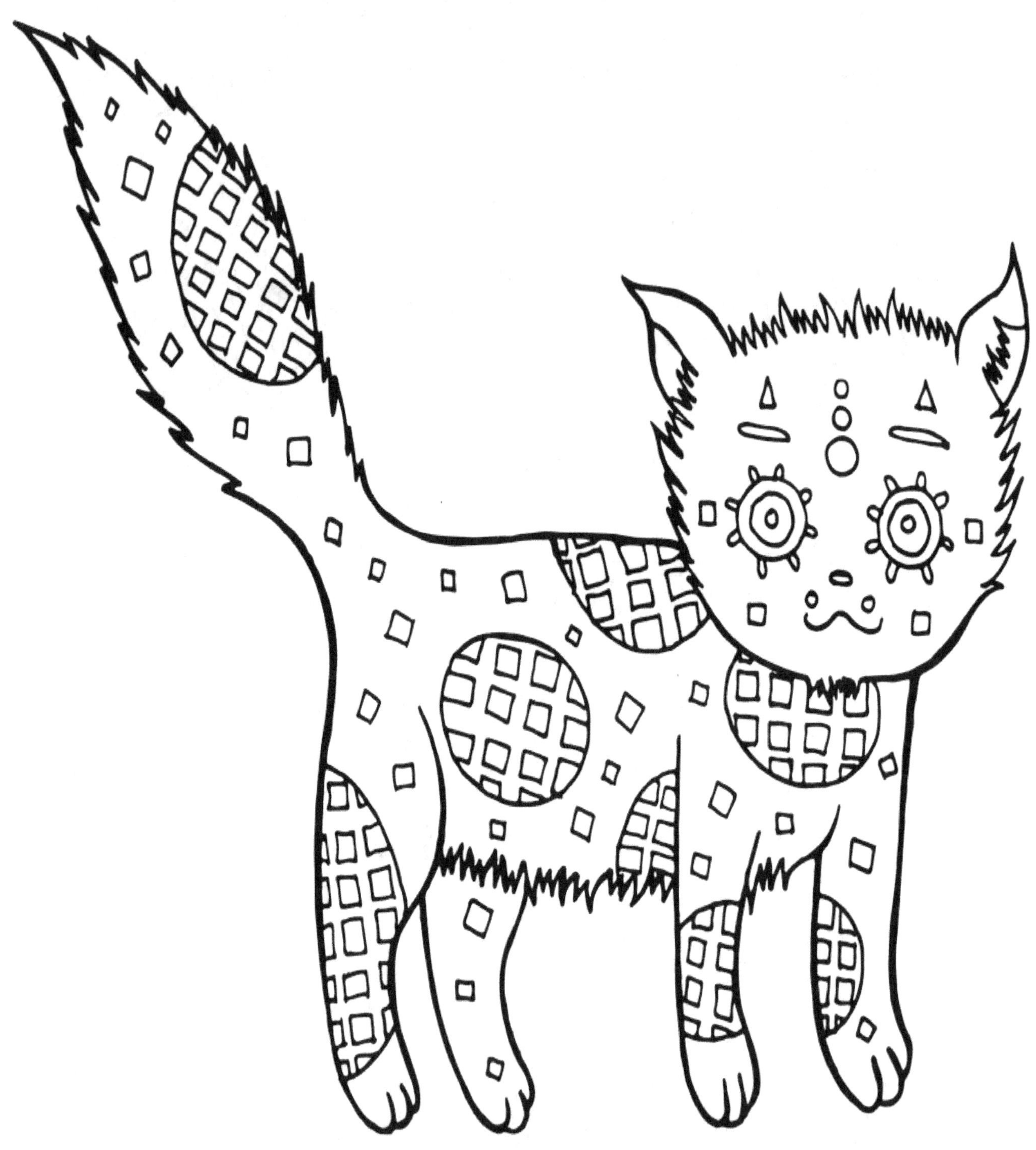

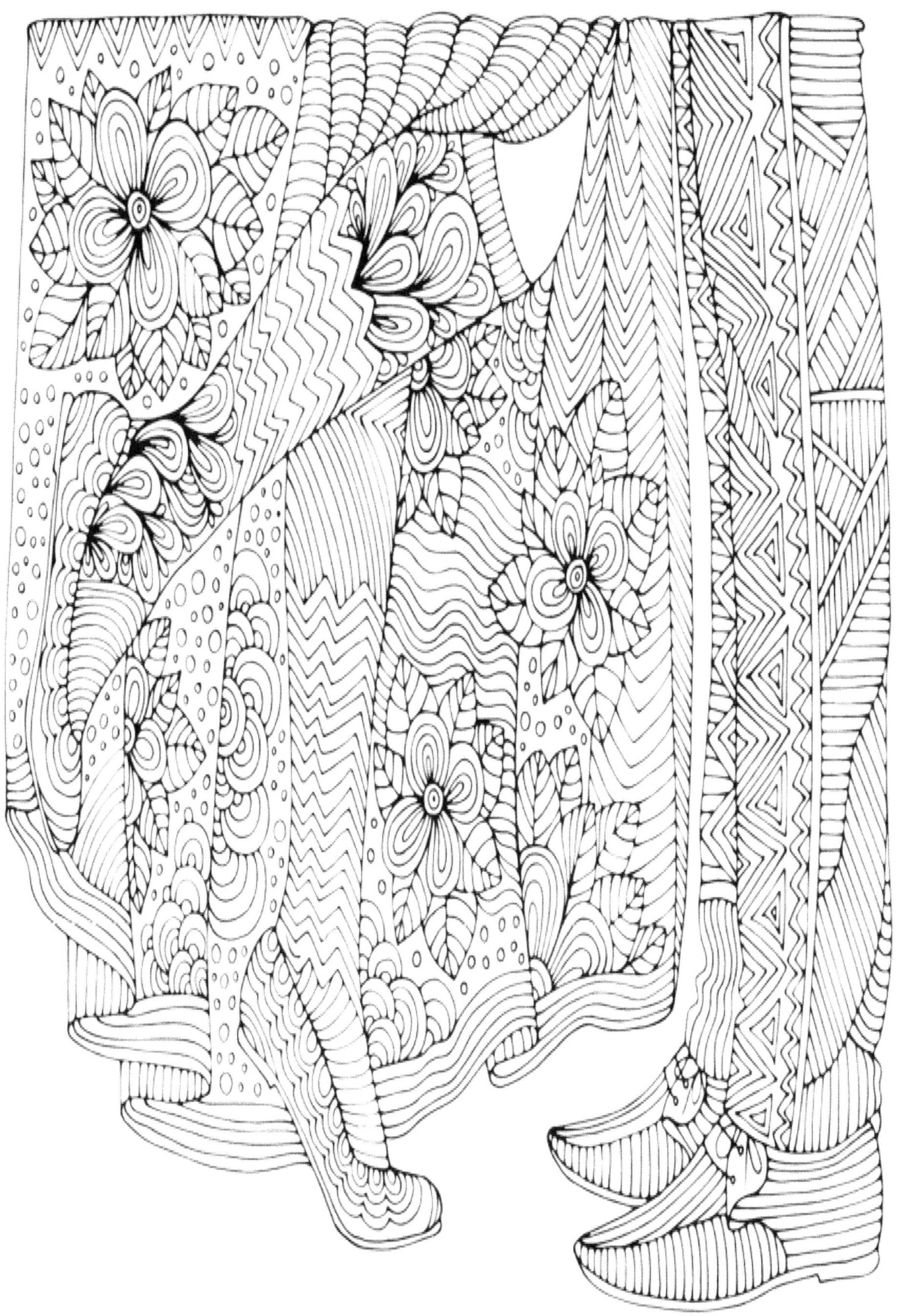

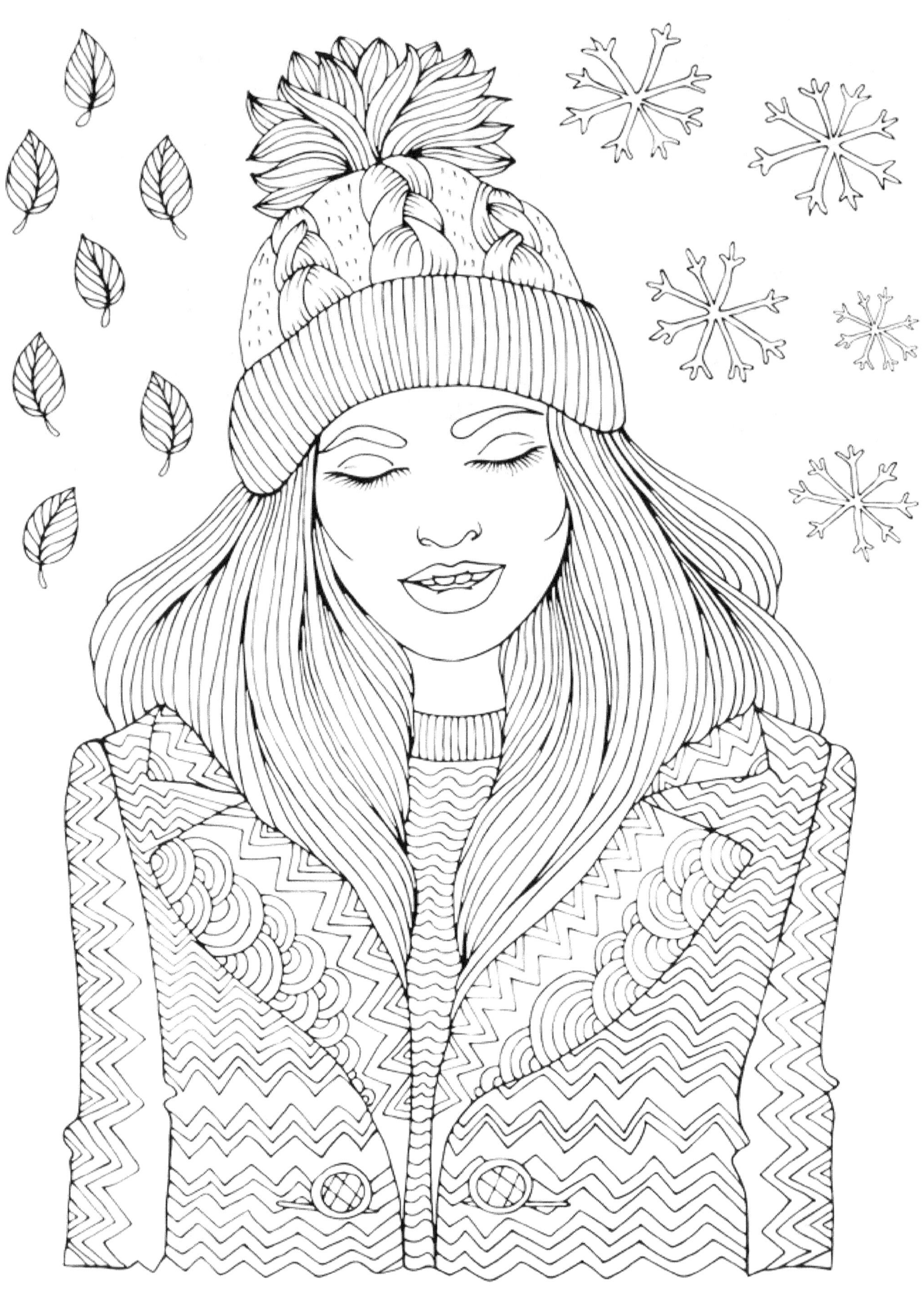

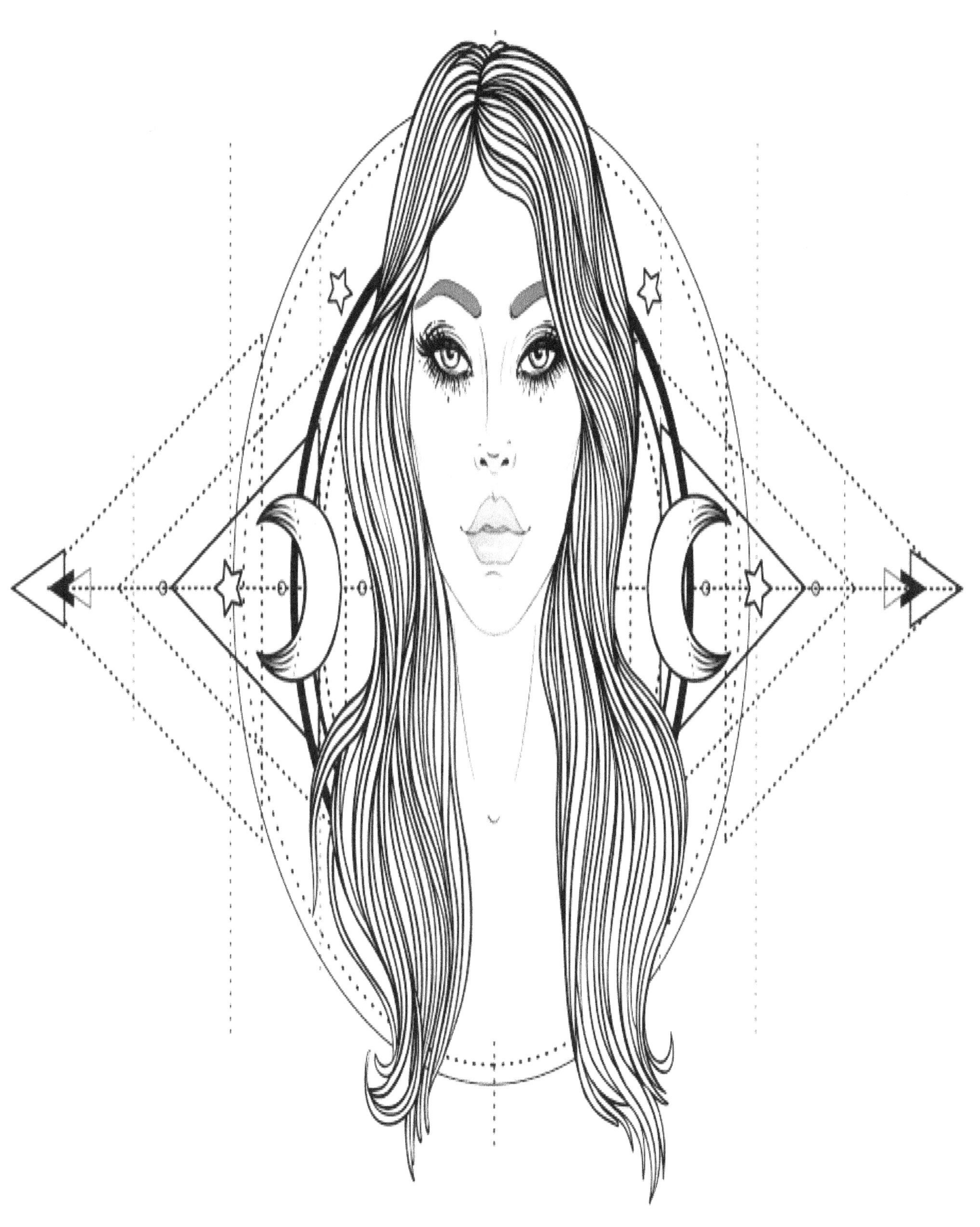

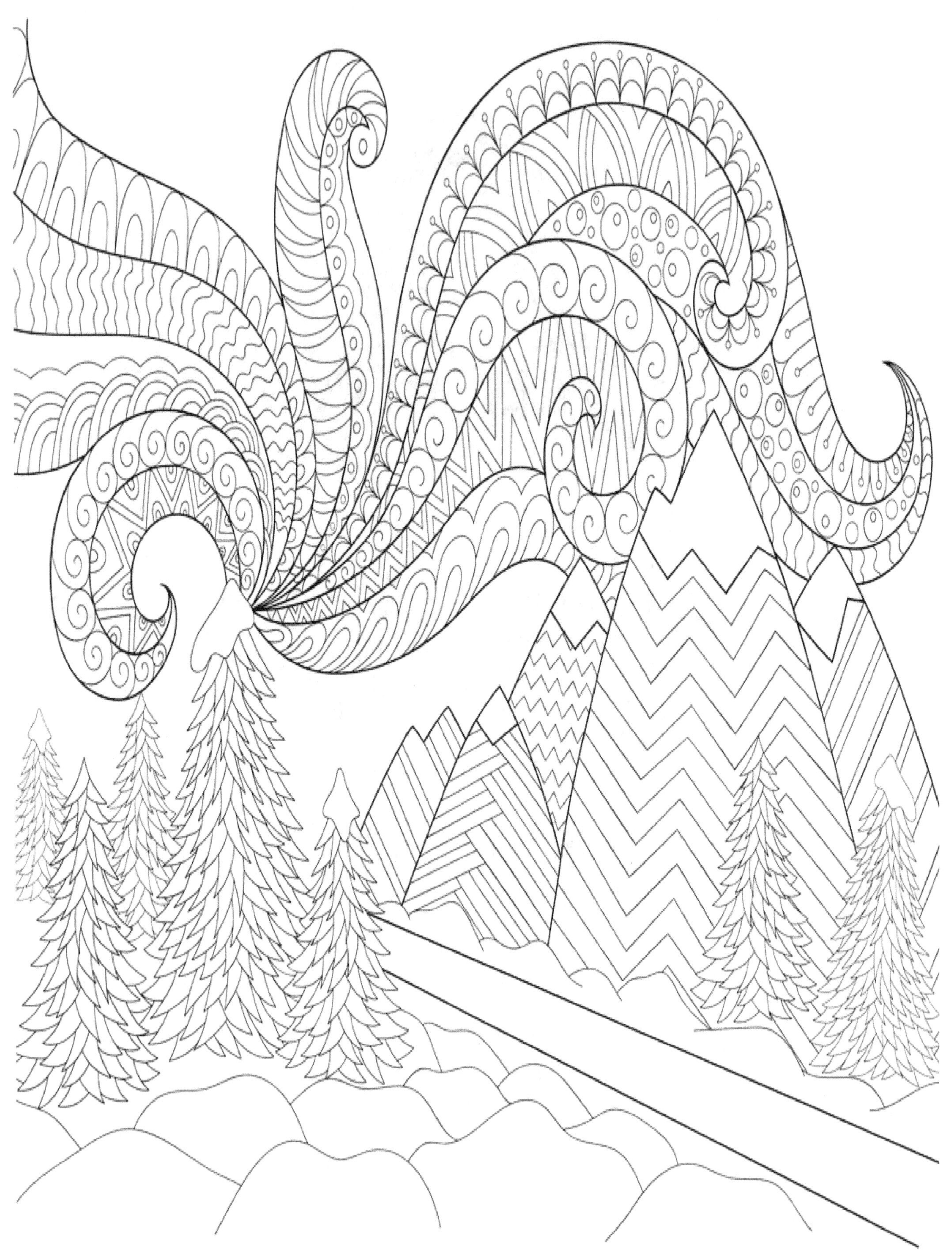

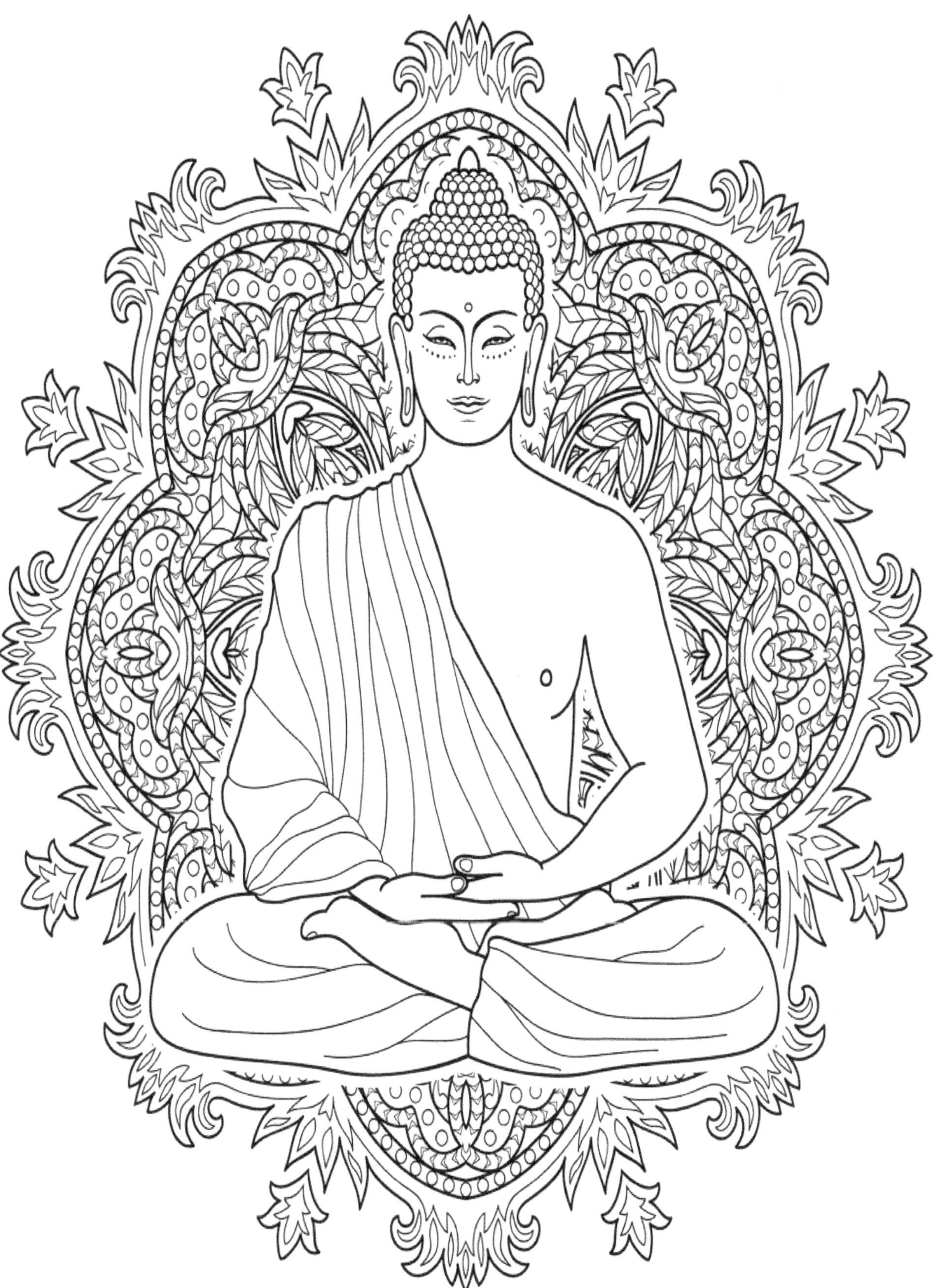

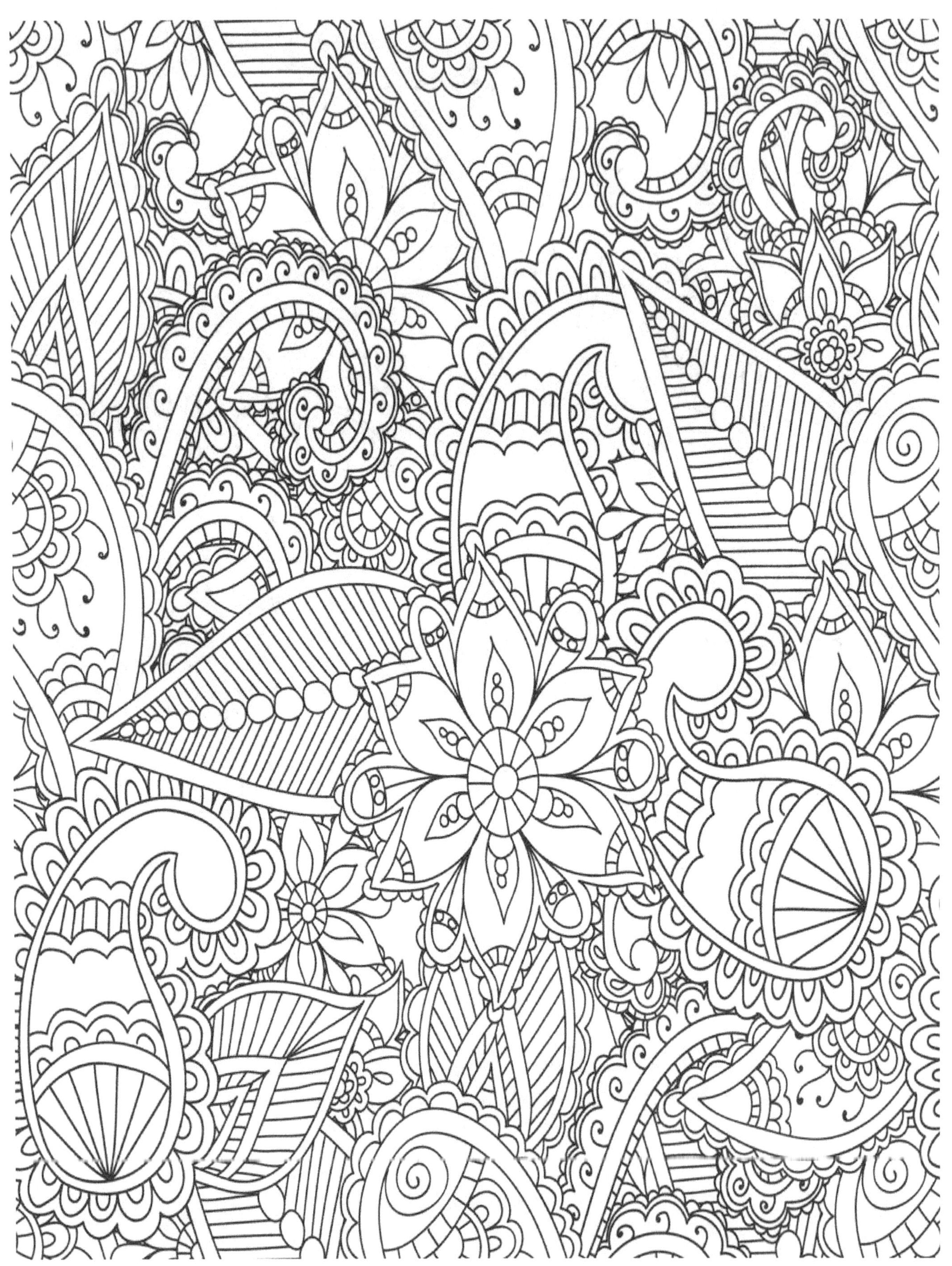

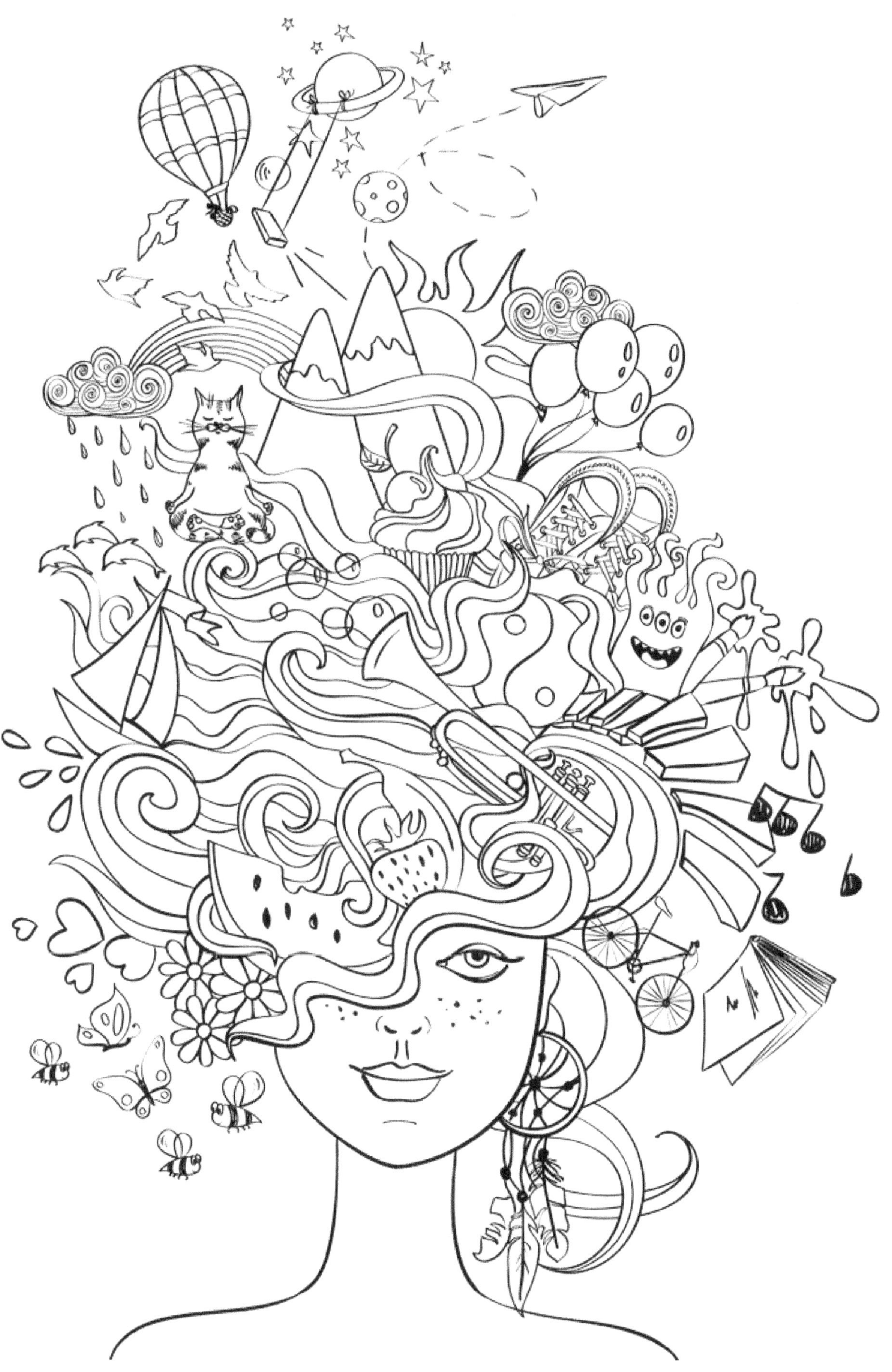

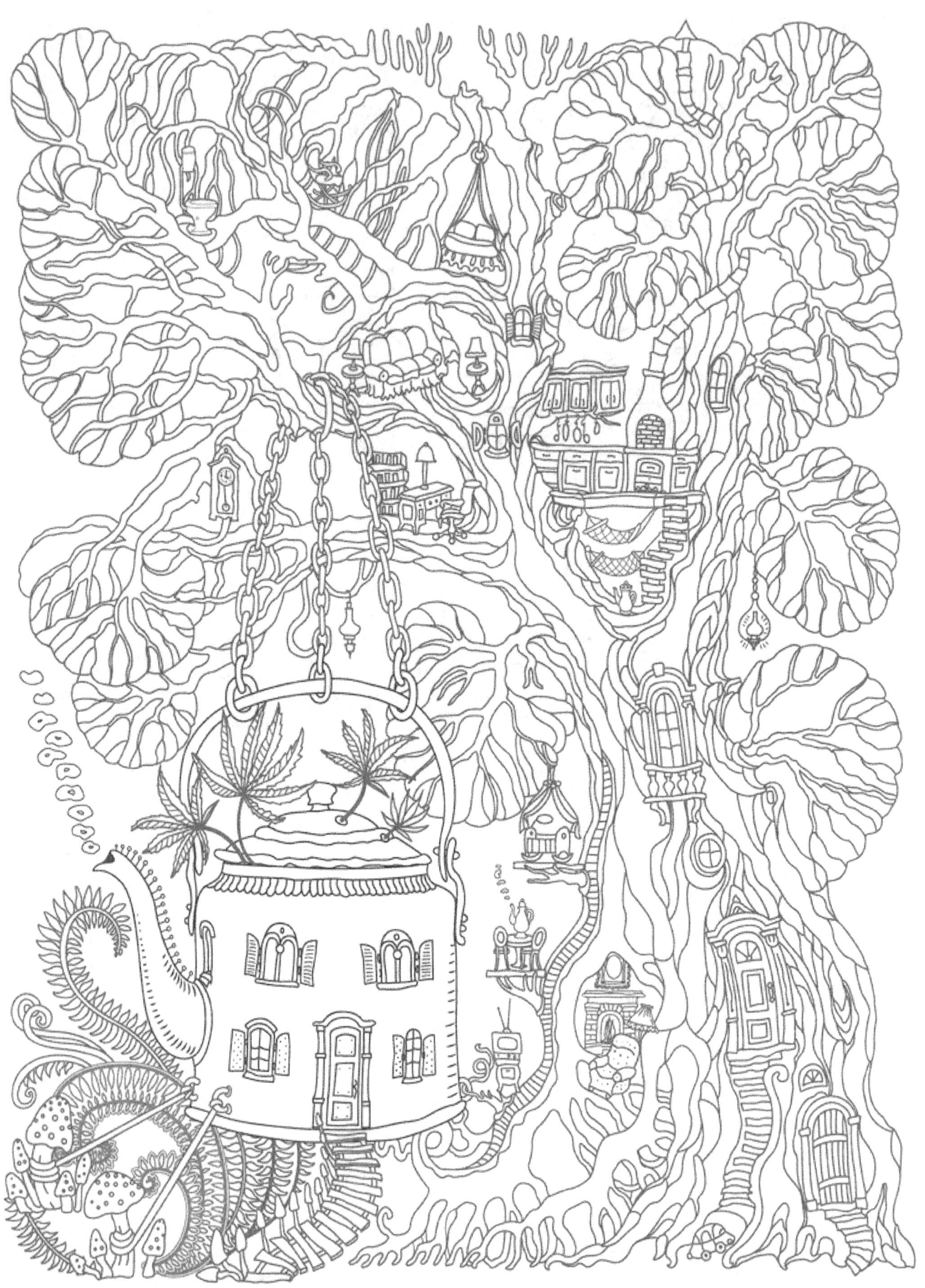

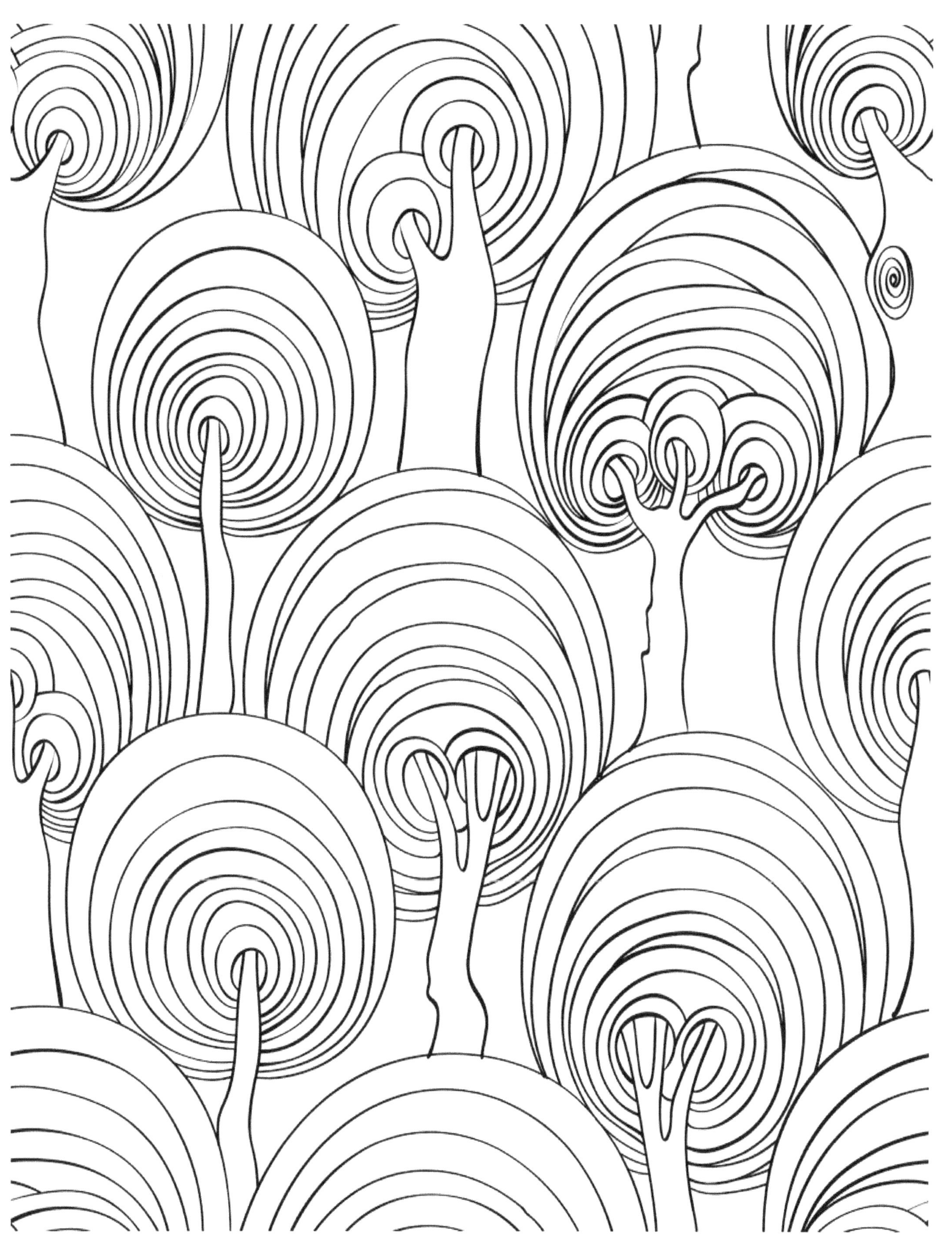

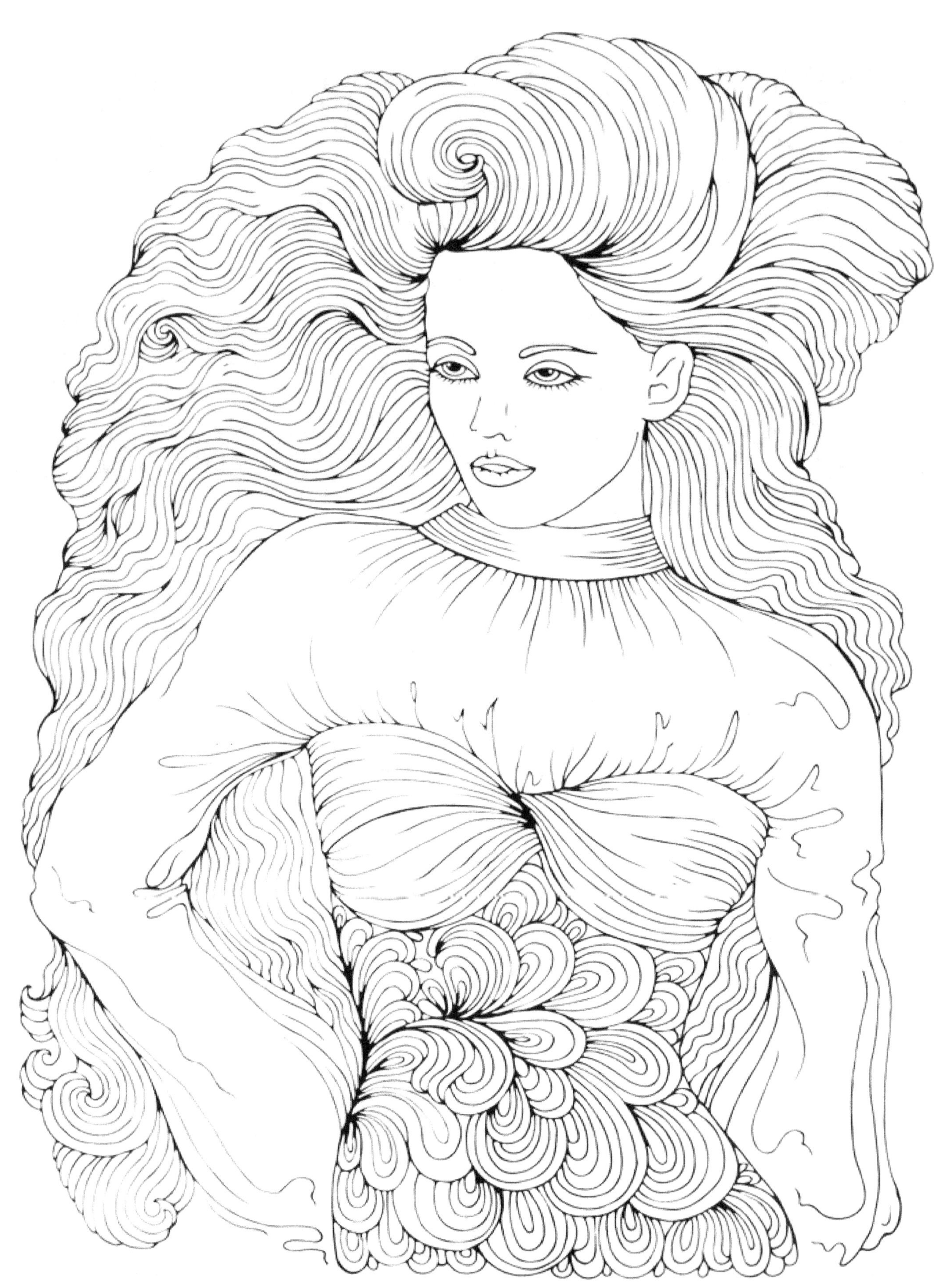

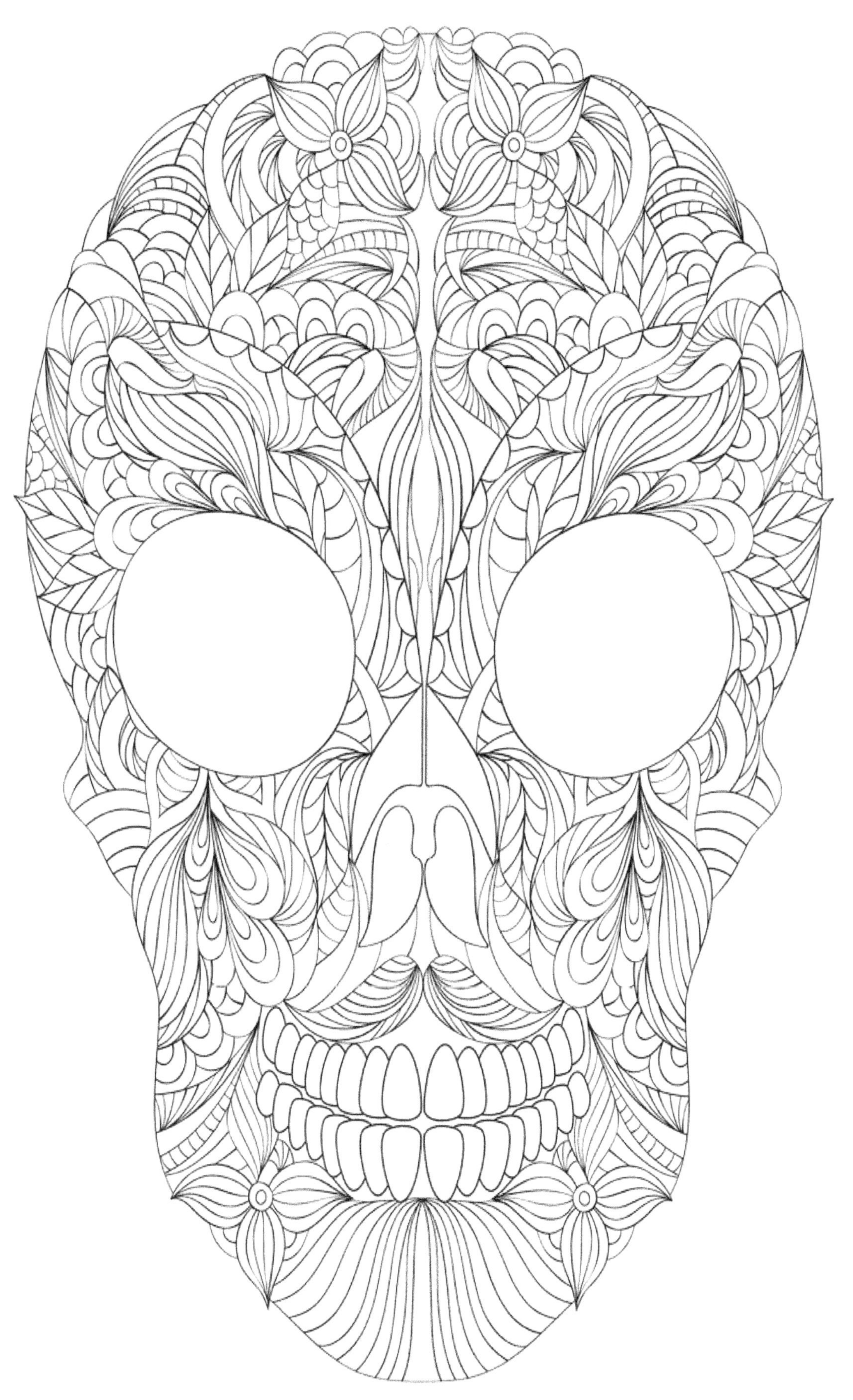

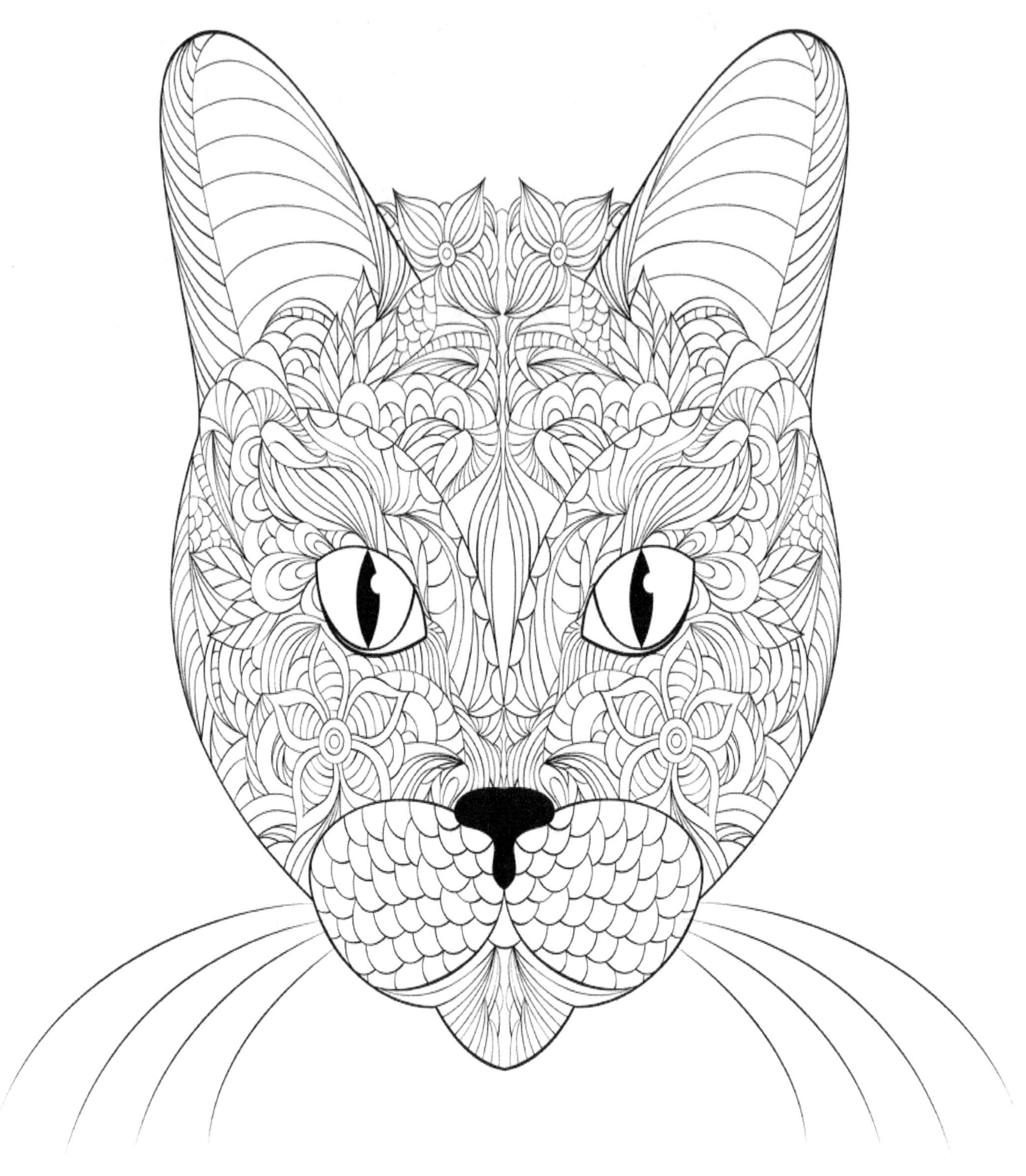

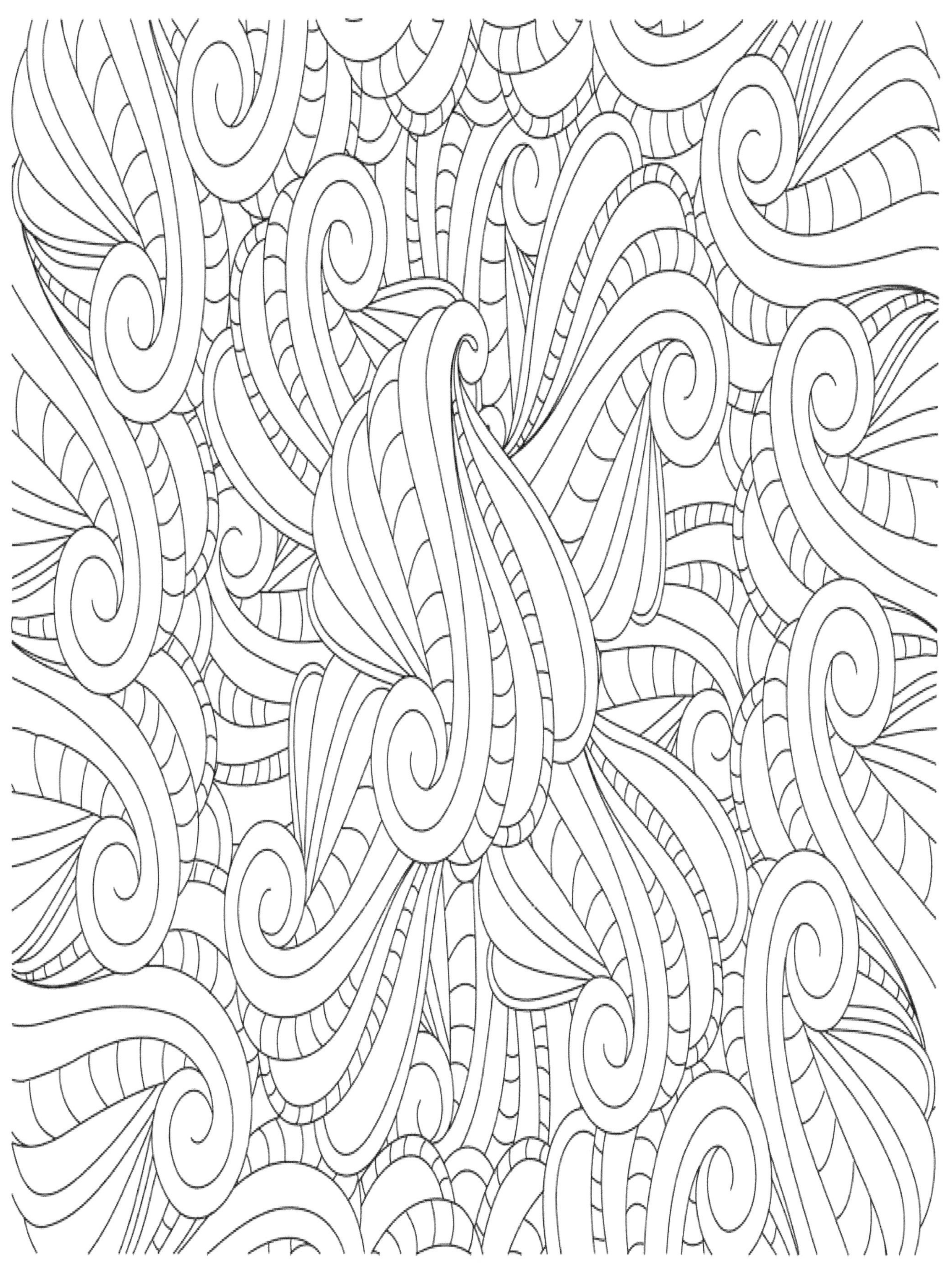

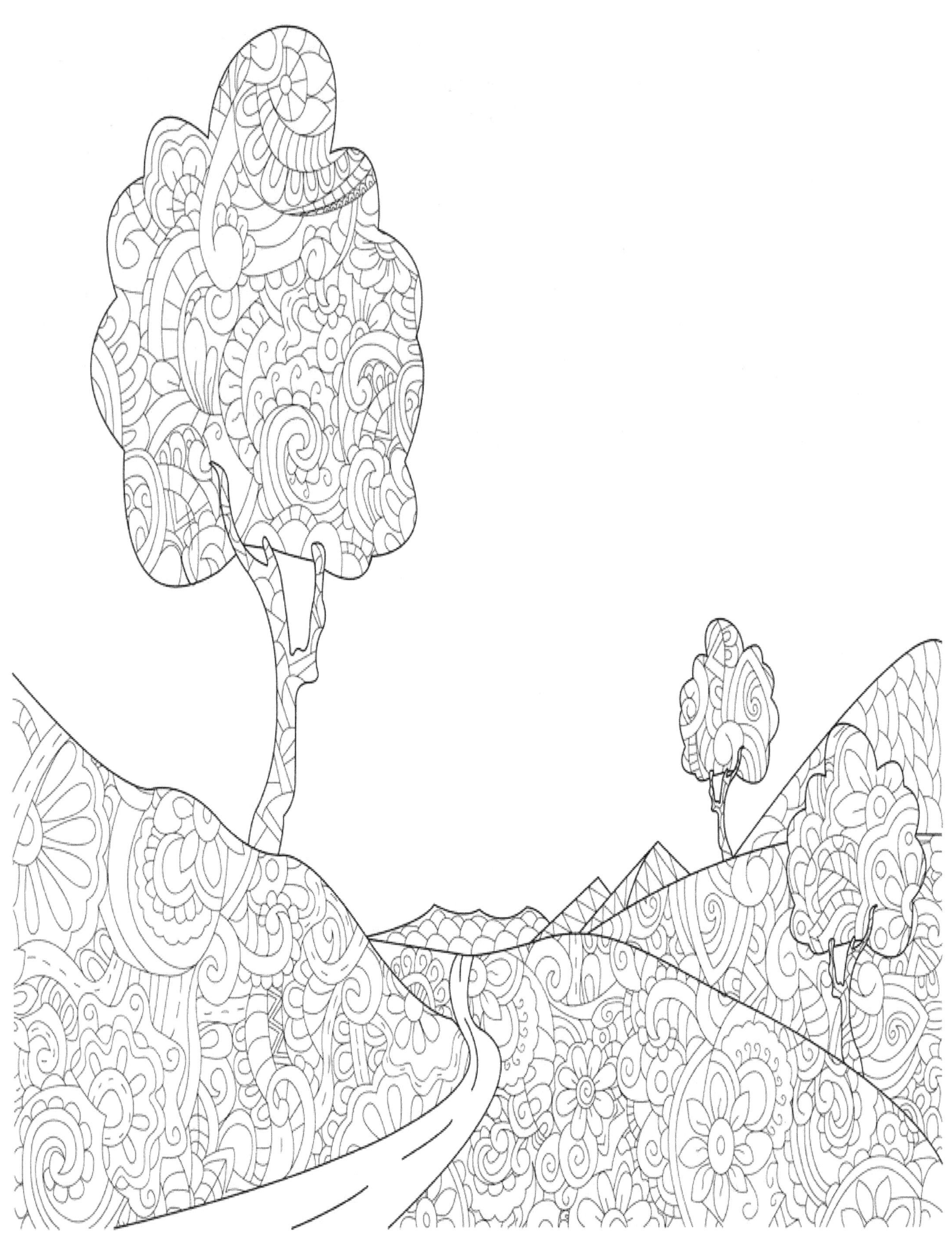

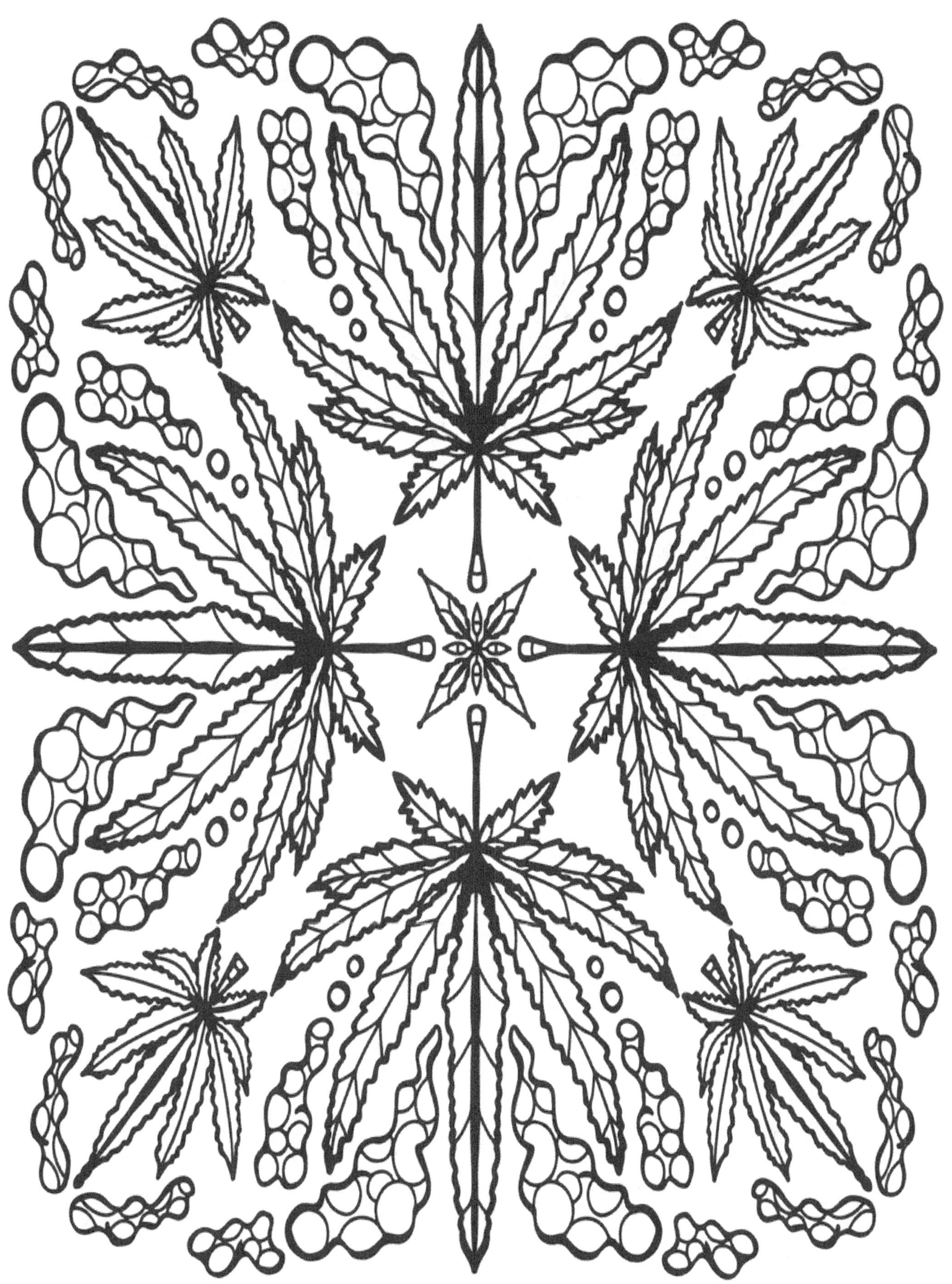

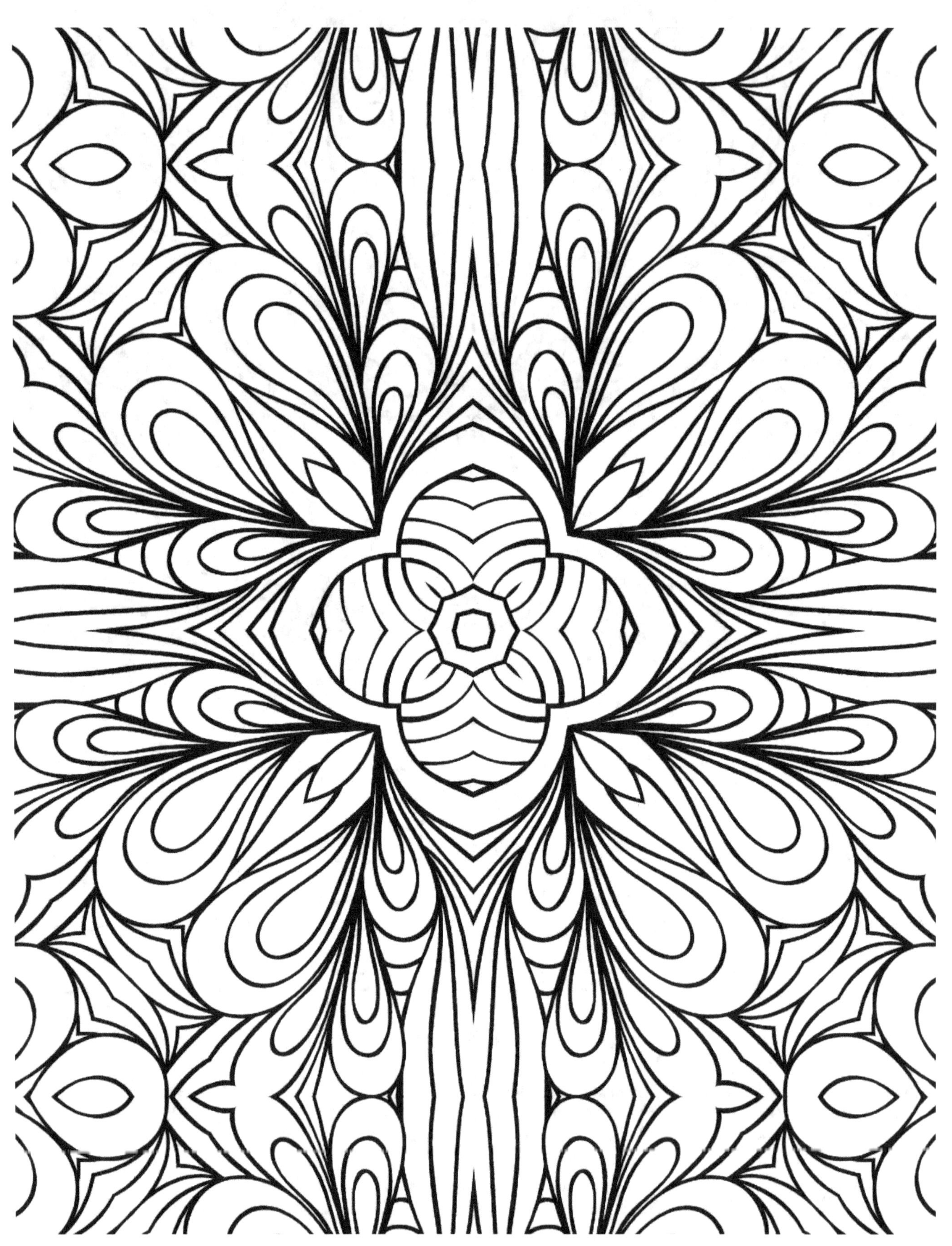

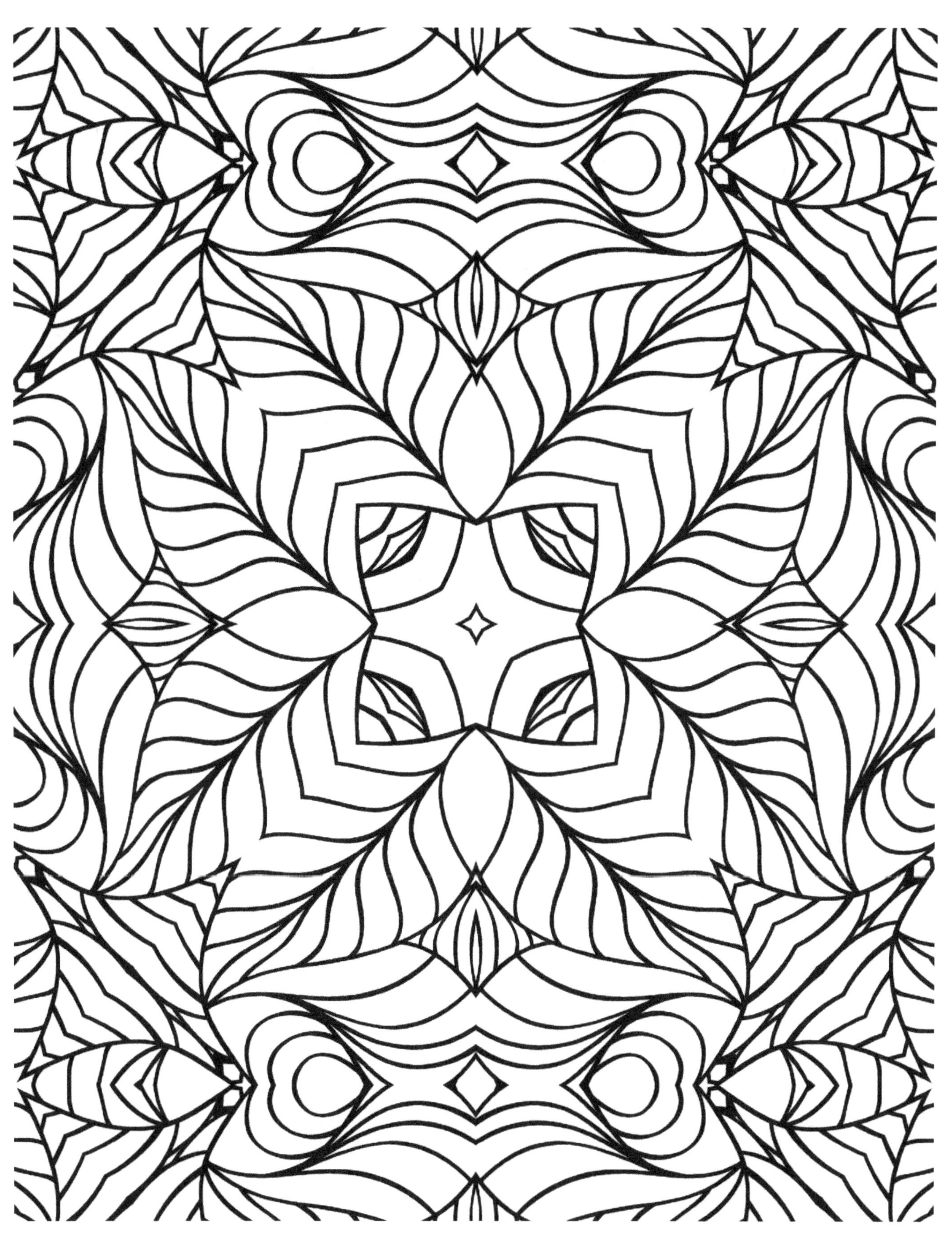

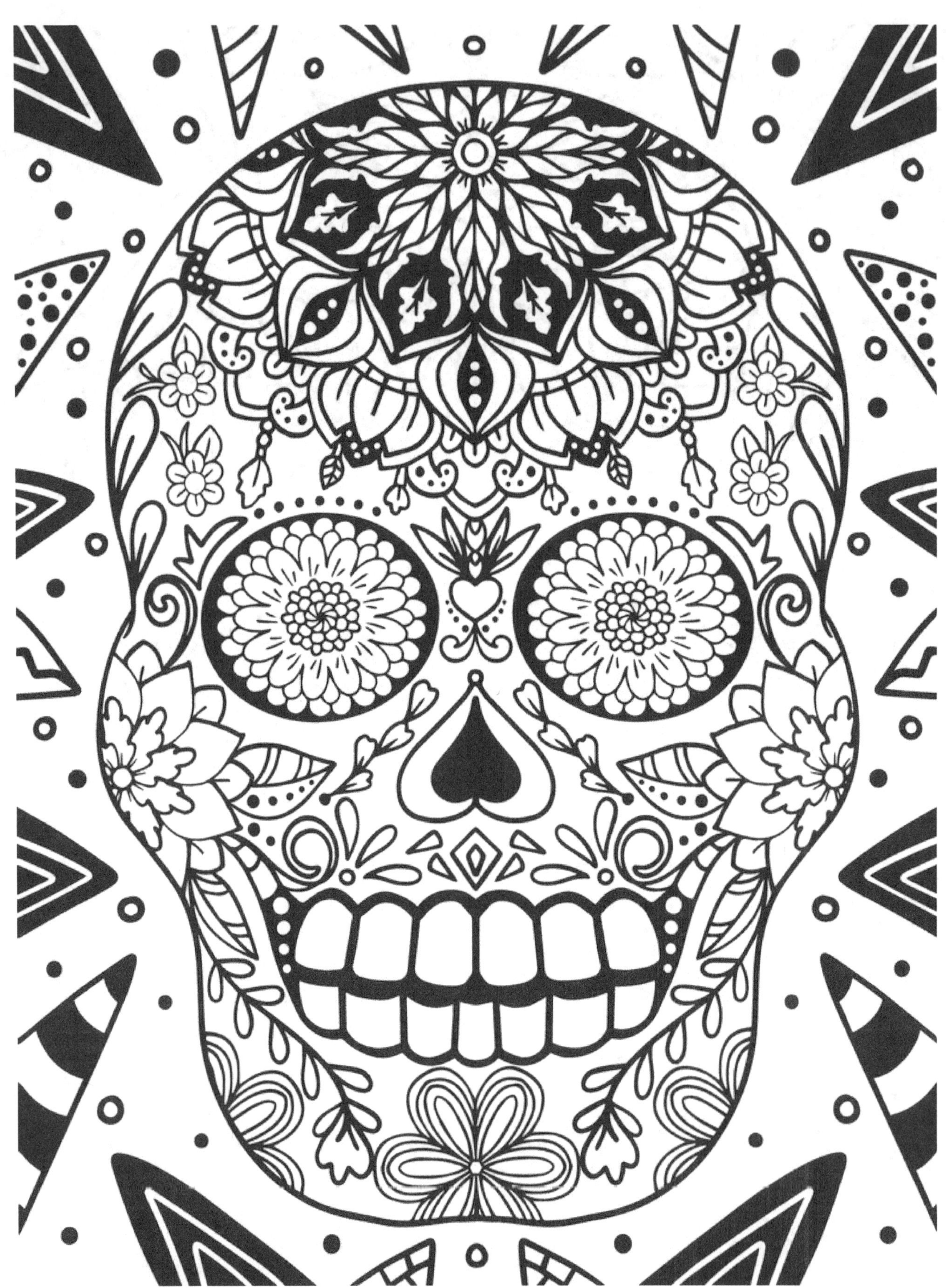

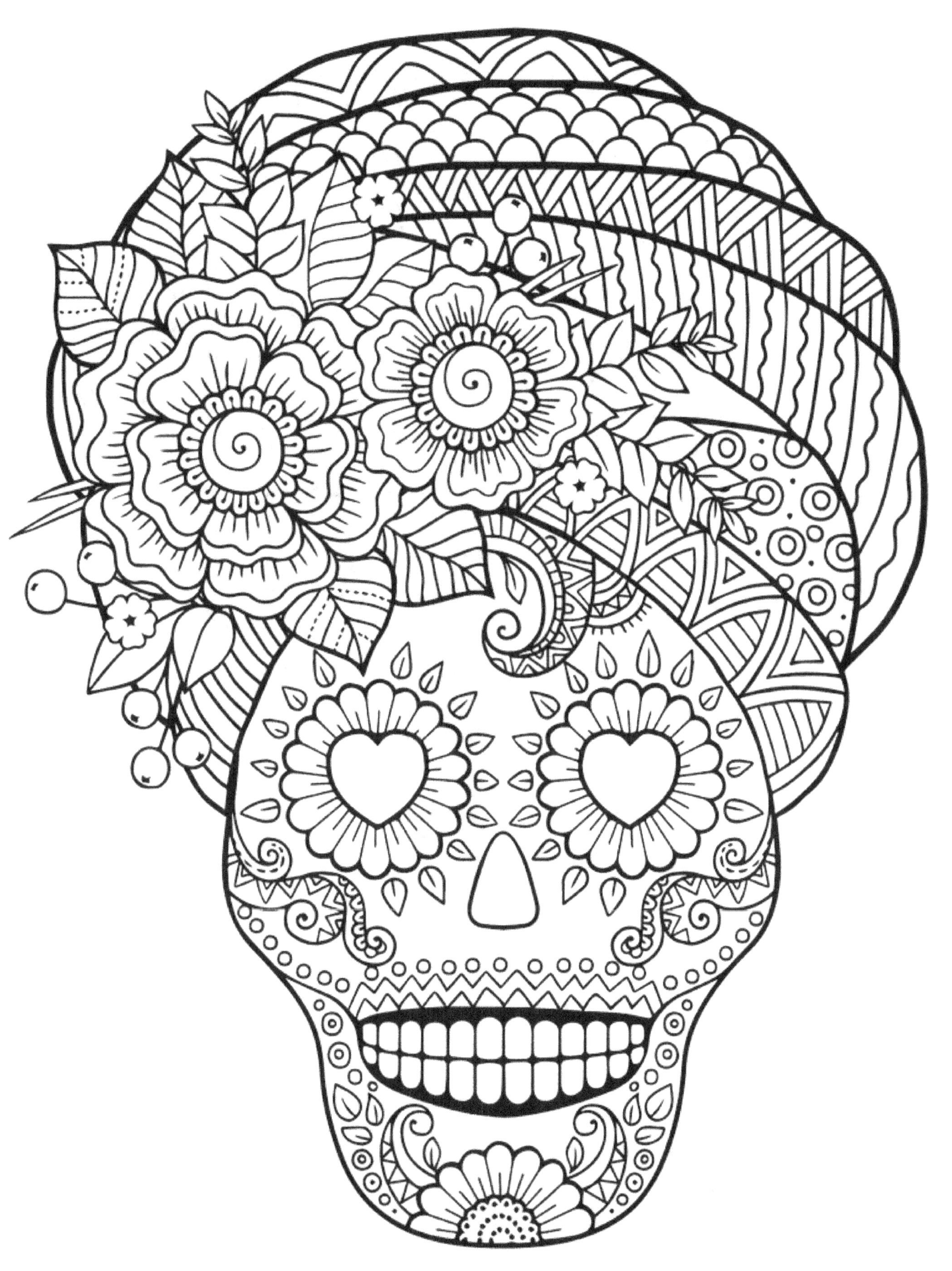

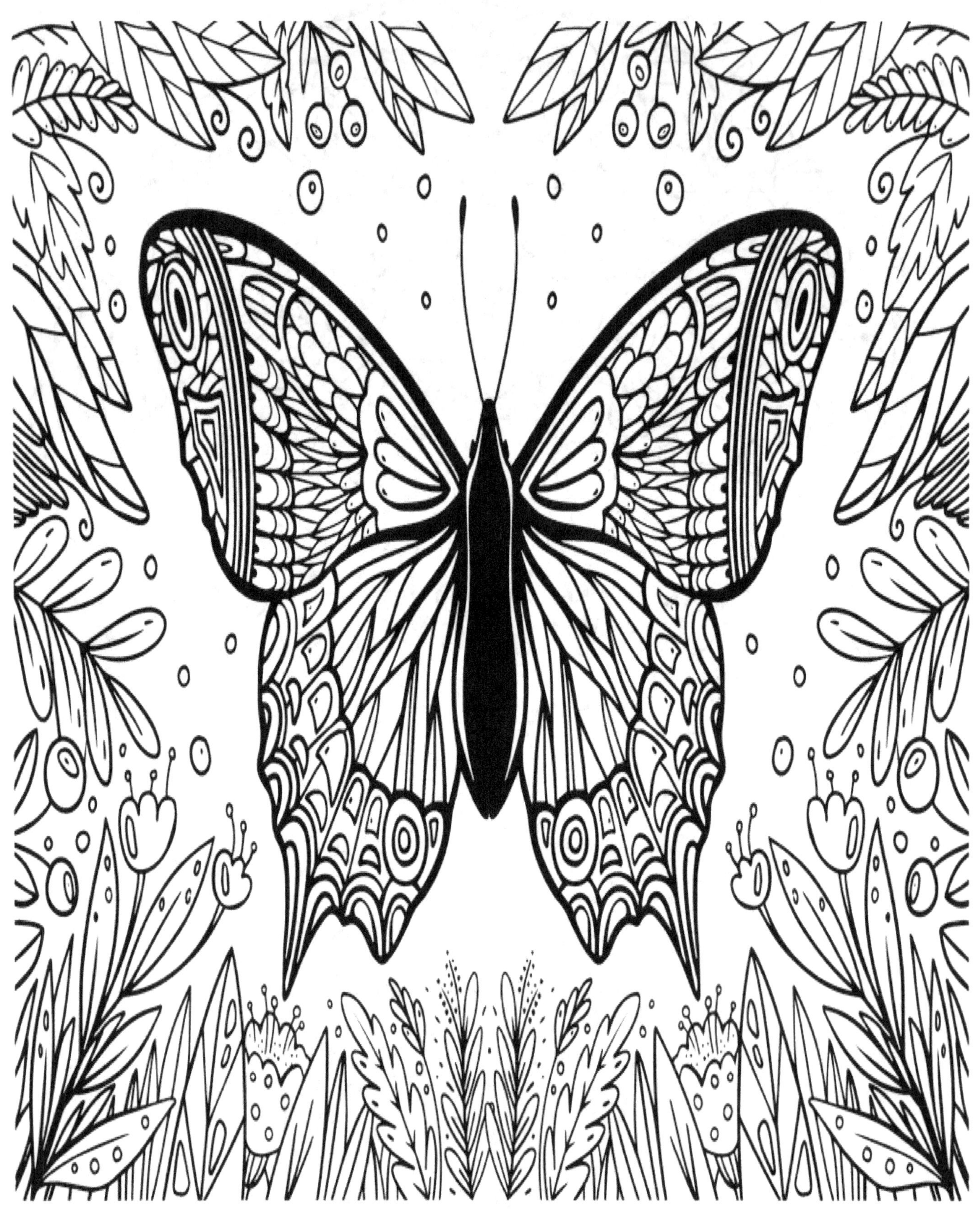

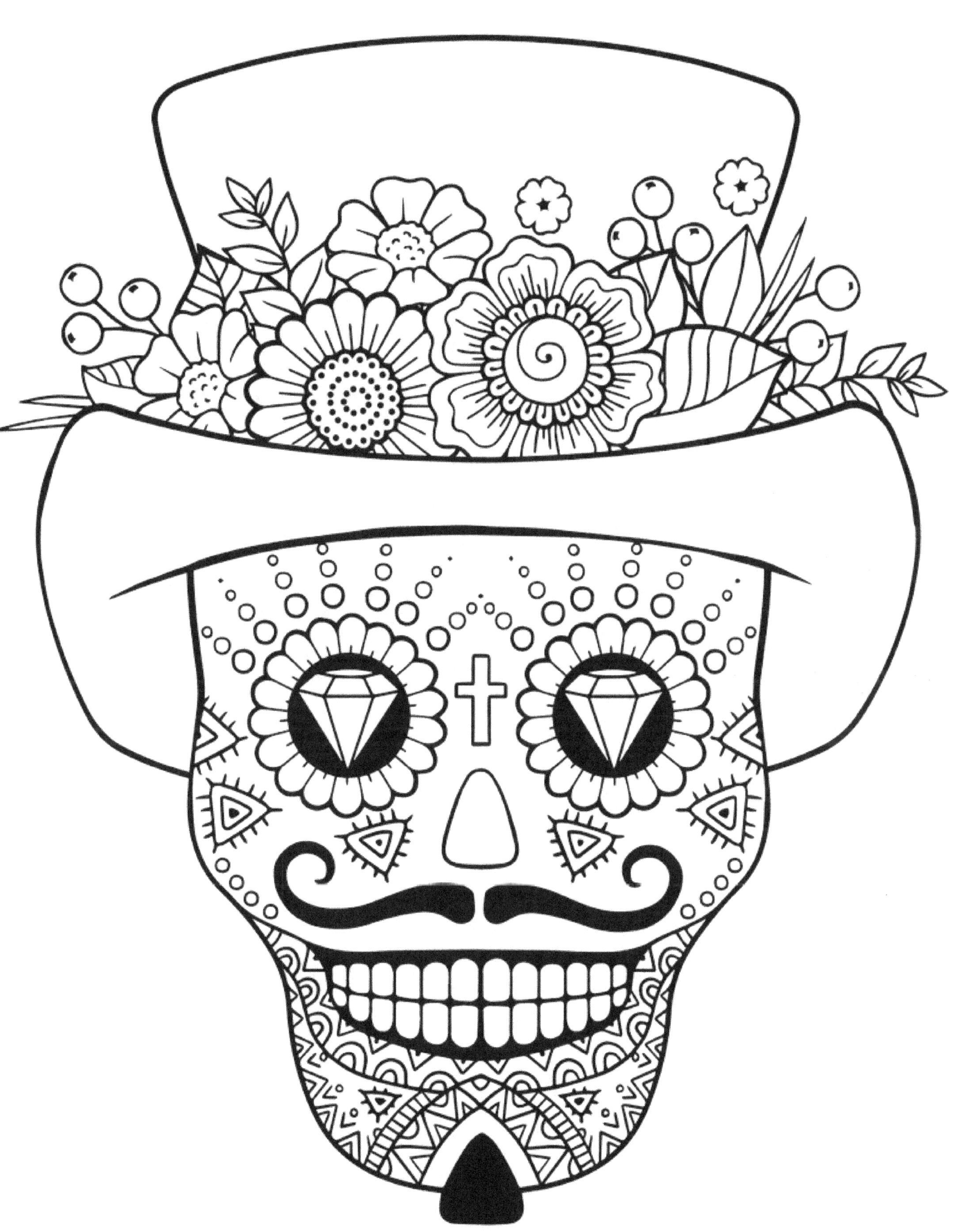

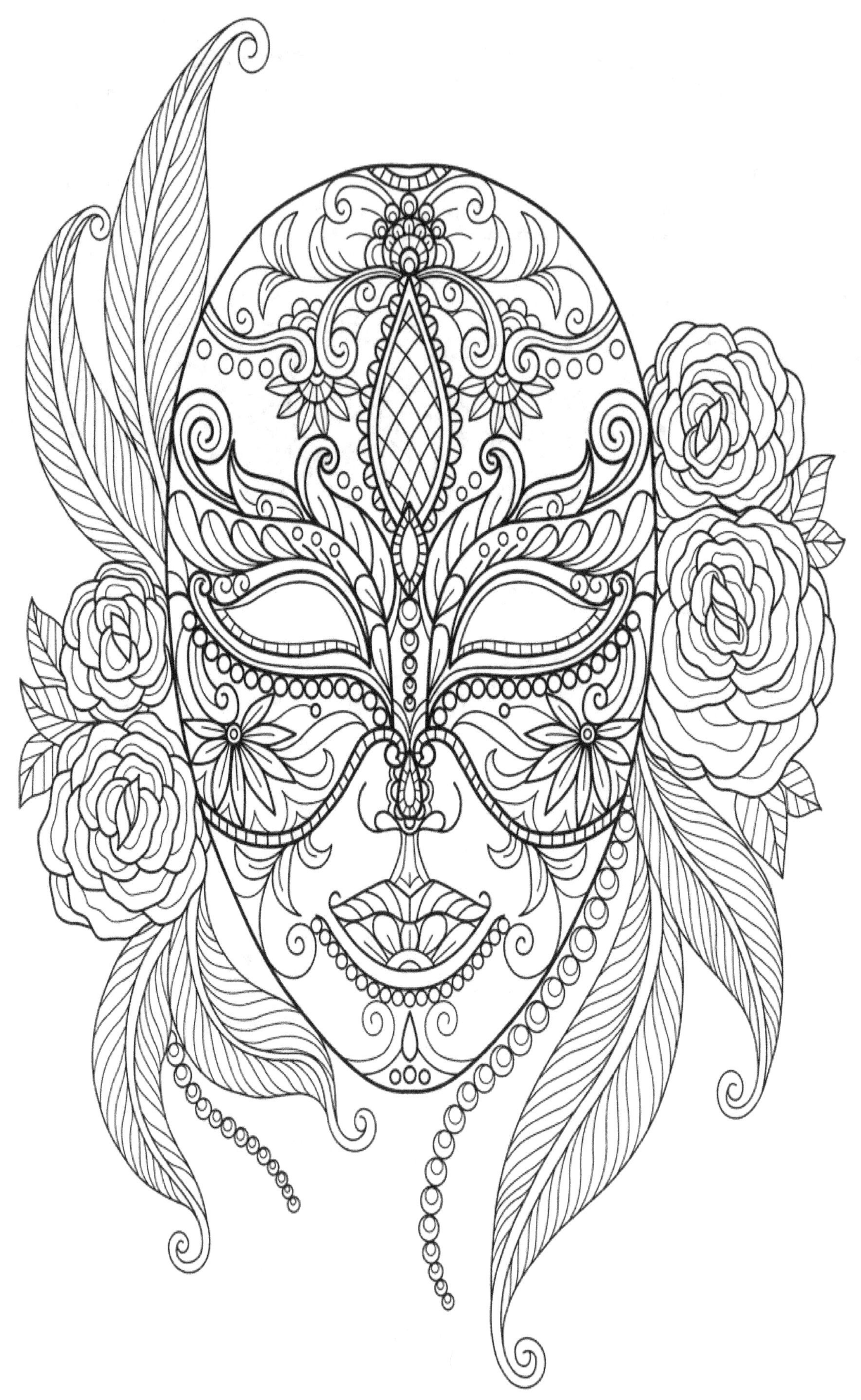

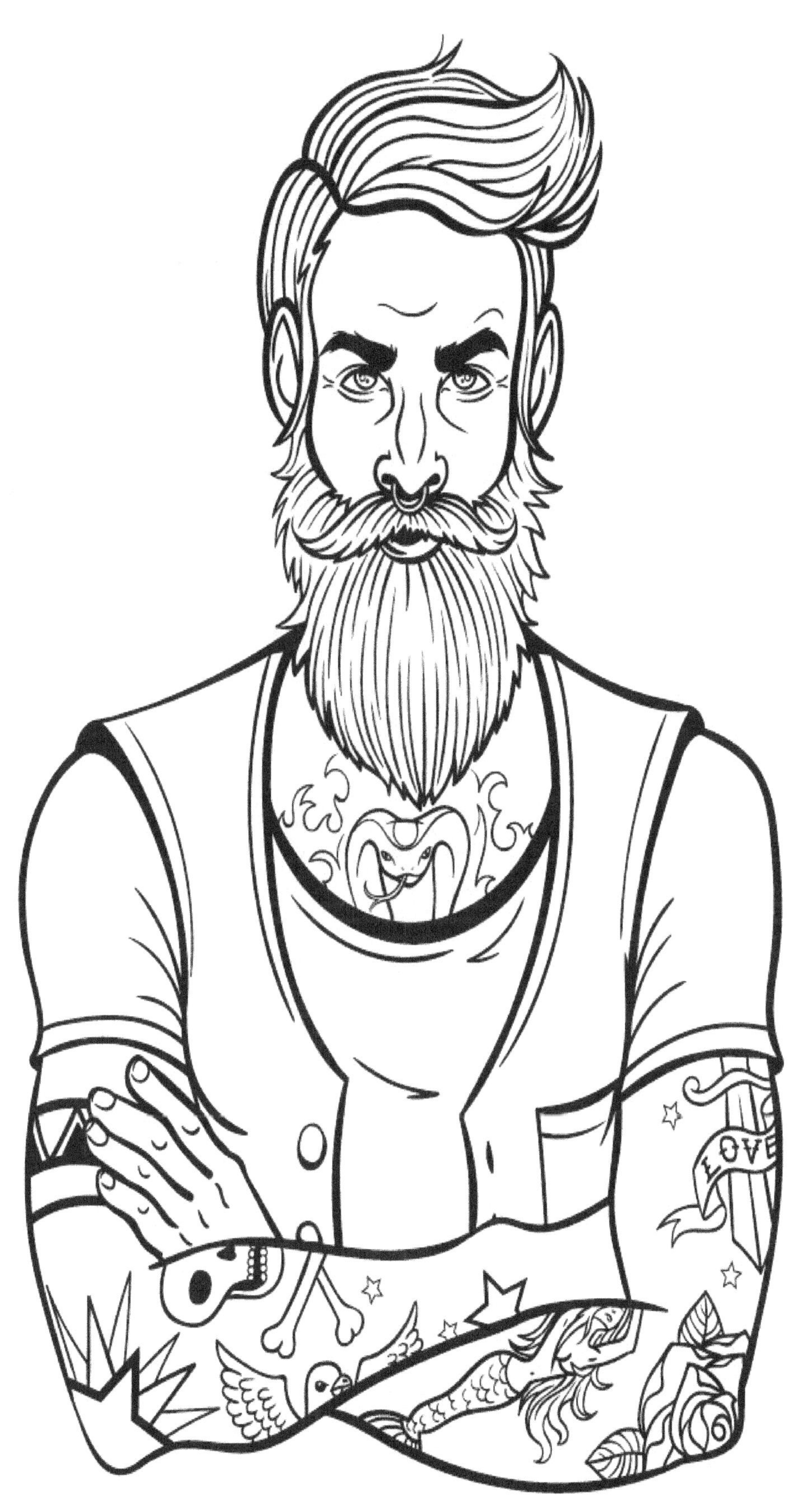

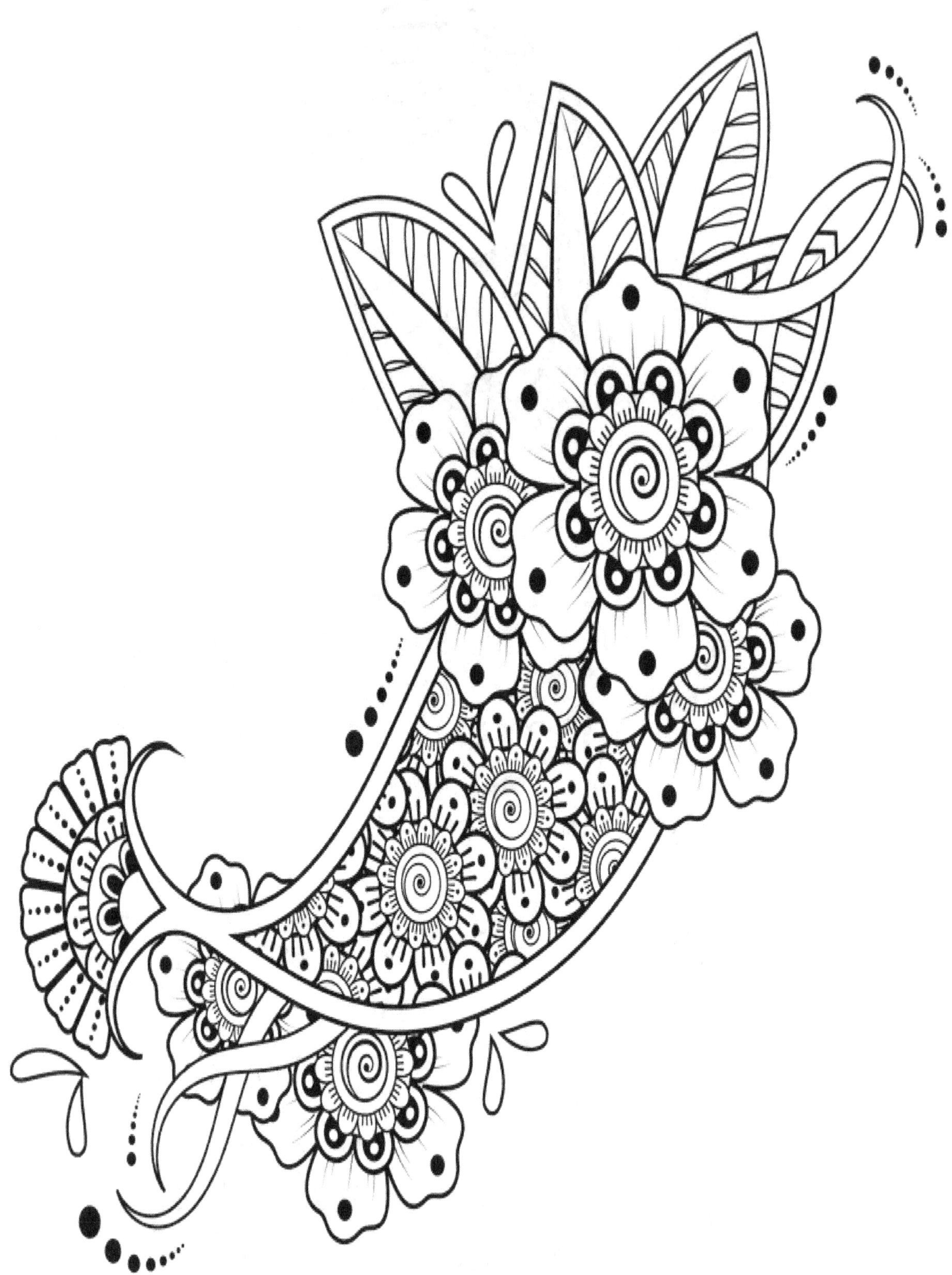

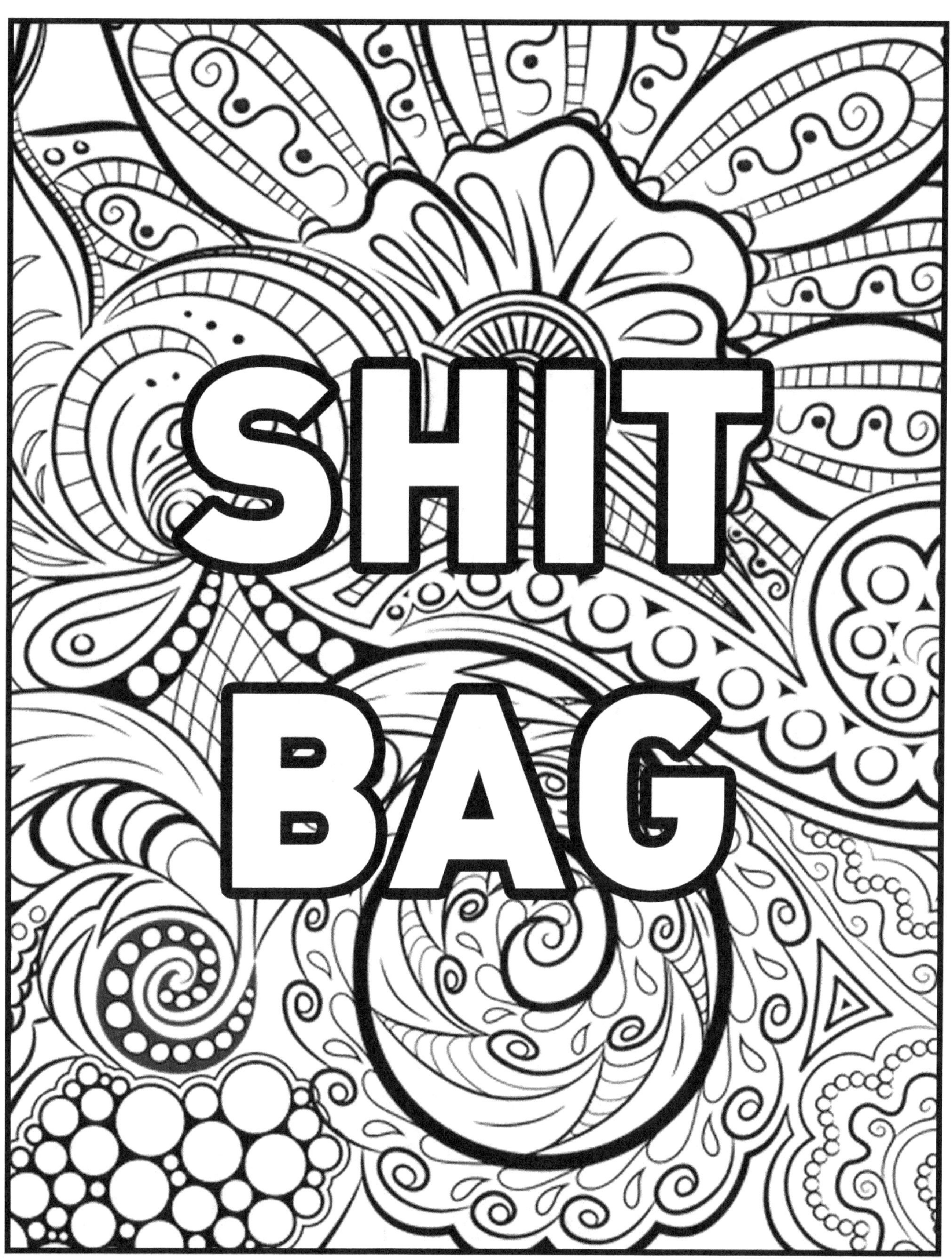
SHIT
BAG

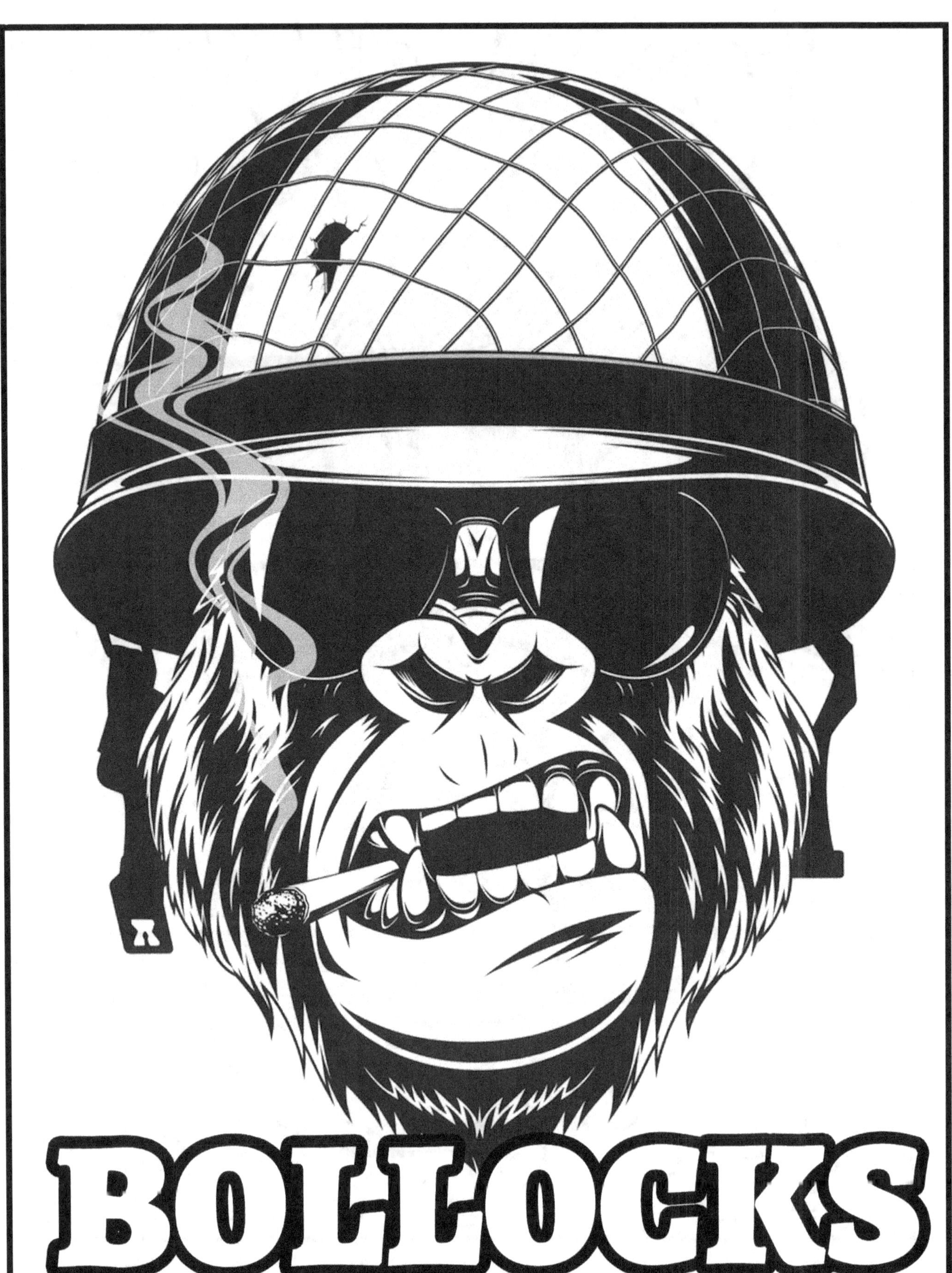

BOLLOCKS

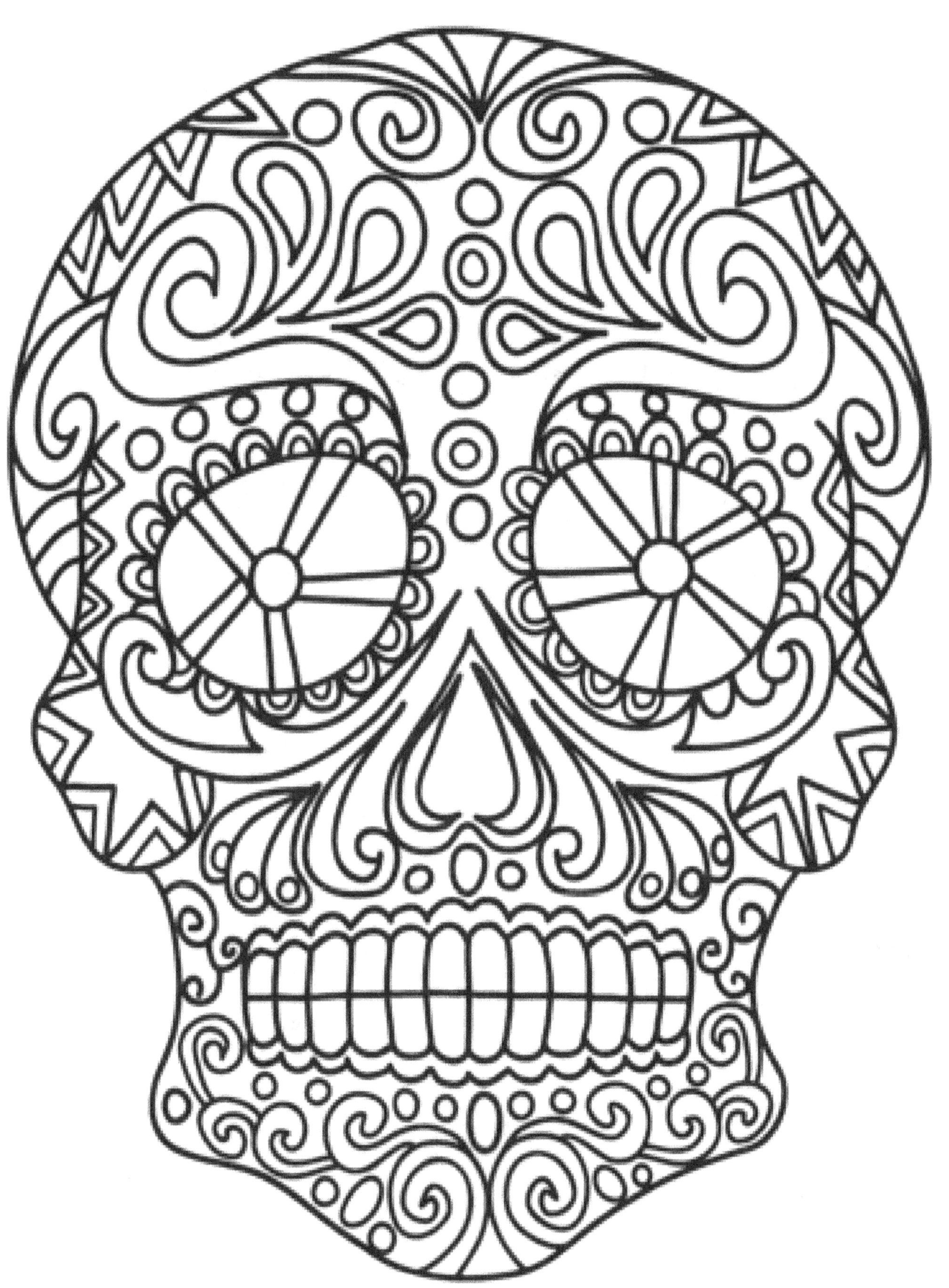

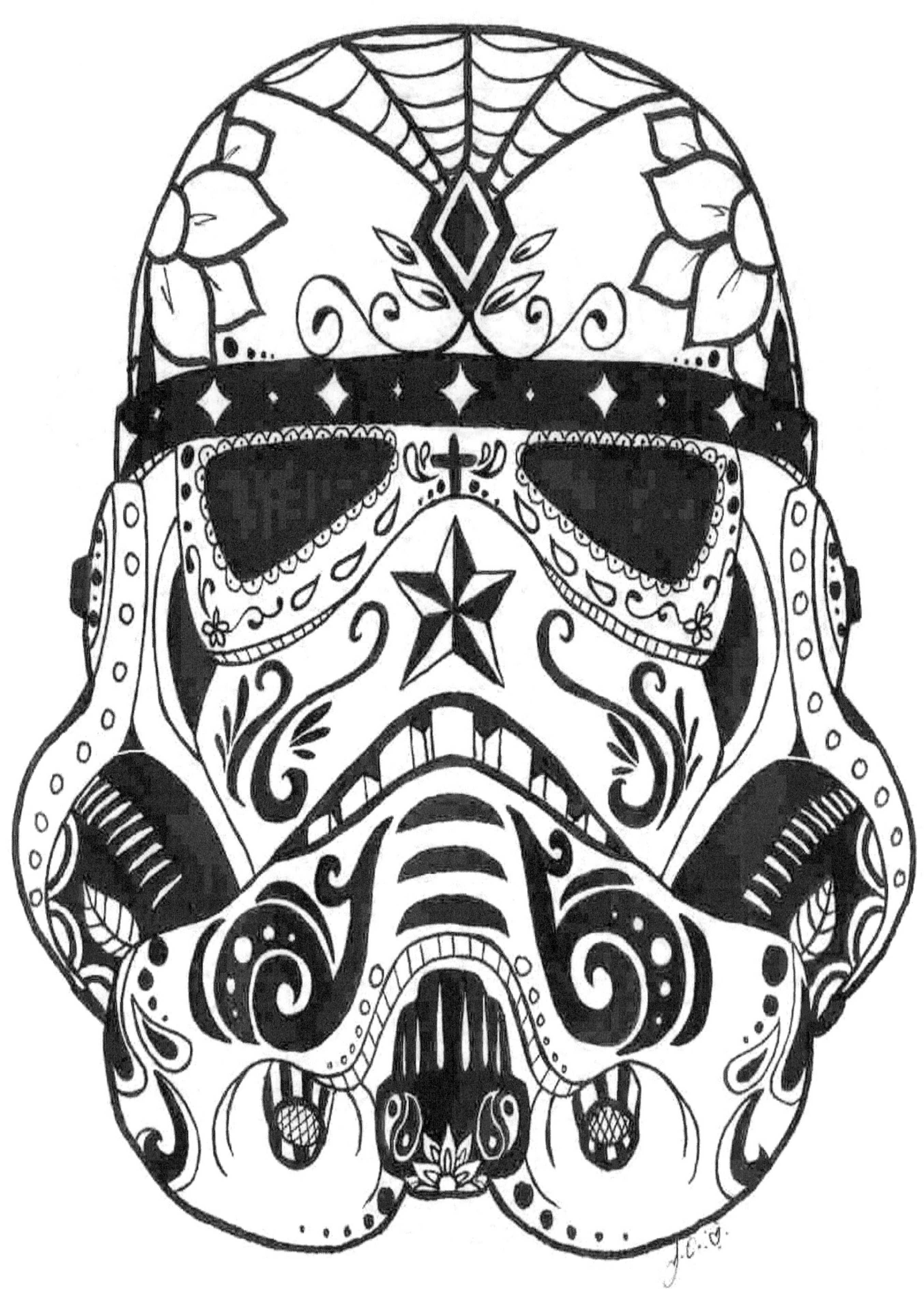

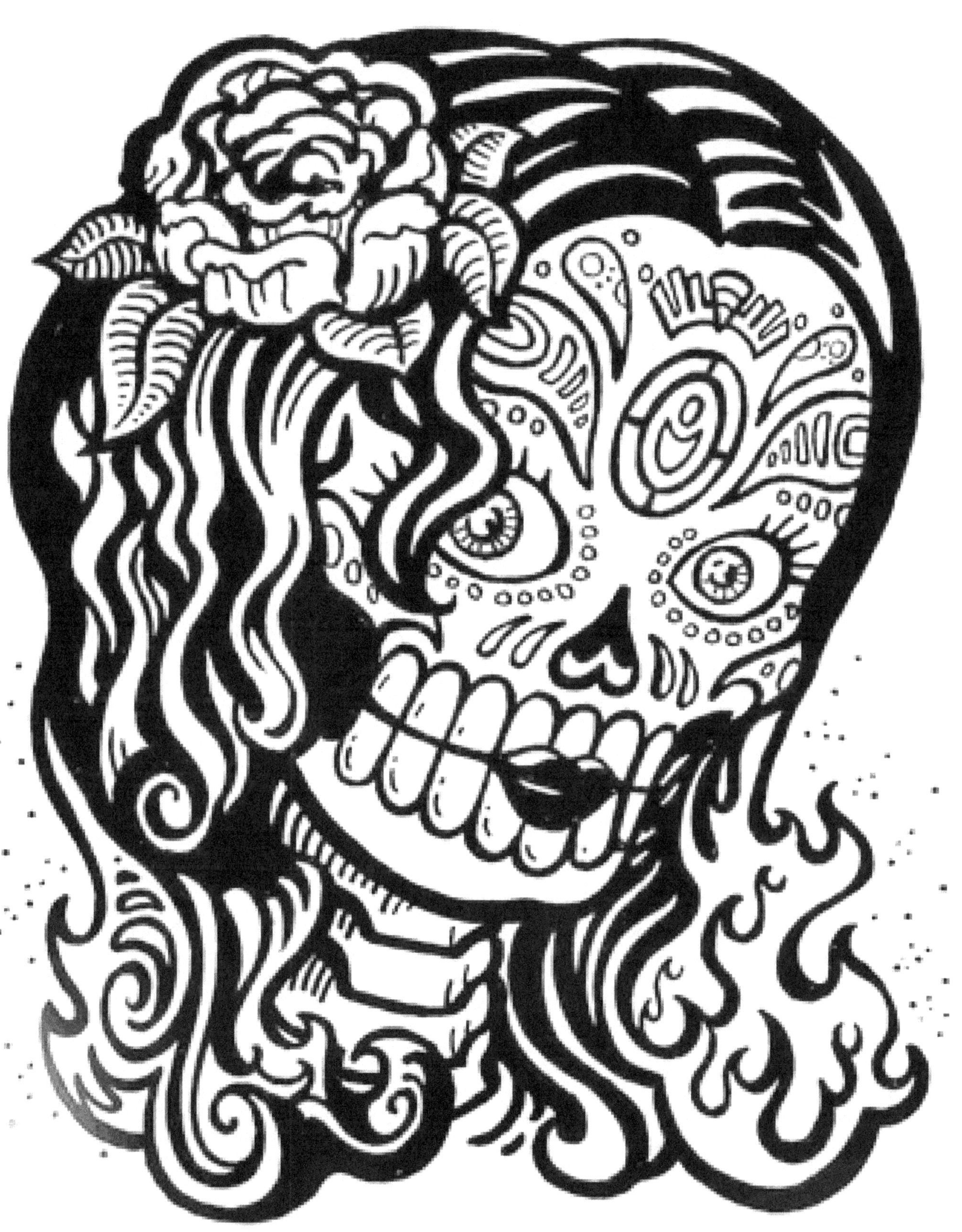

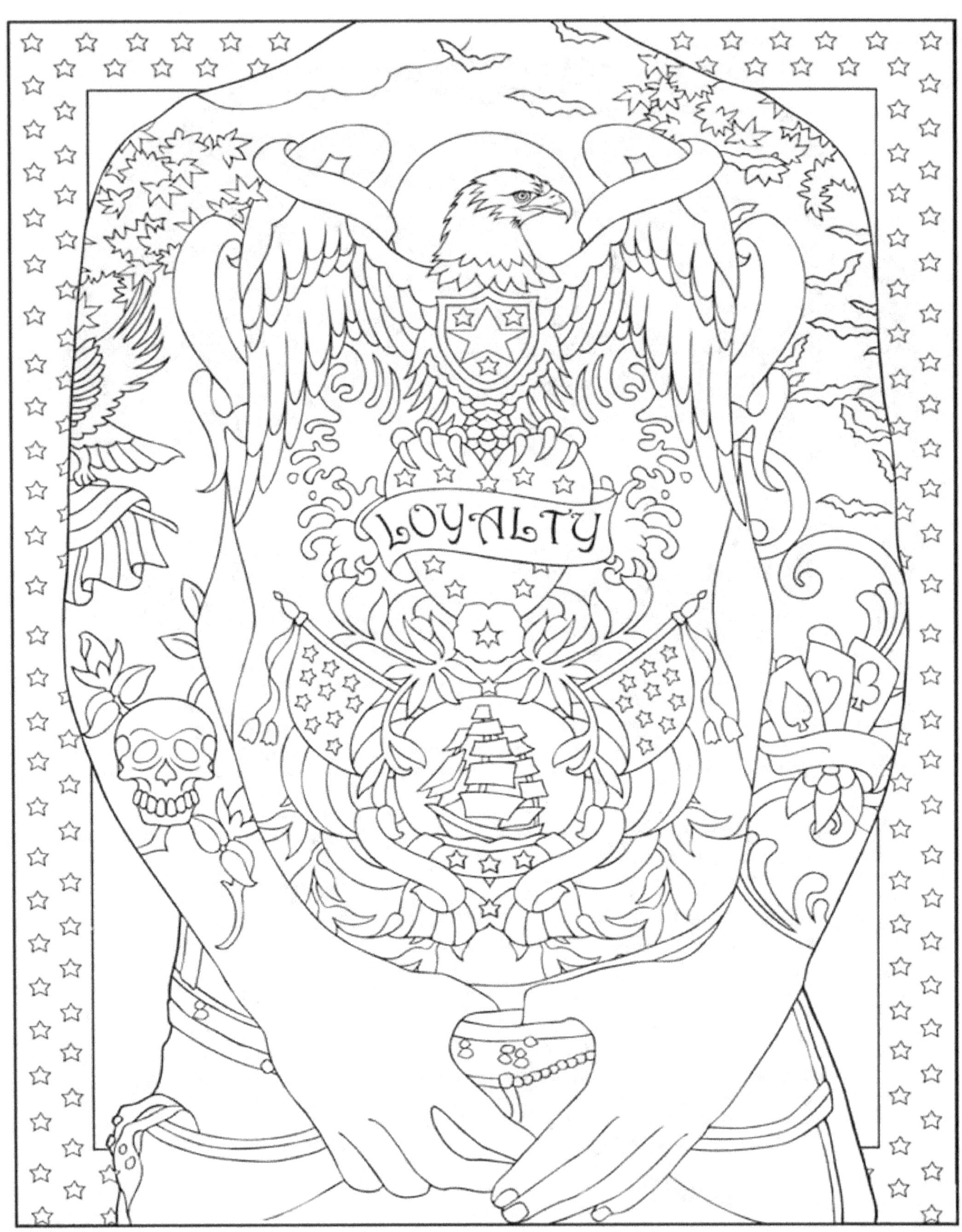
LOYALTY

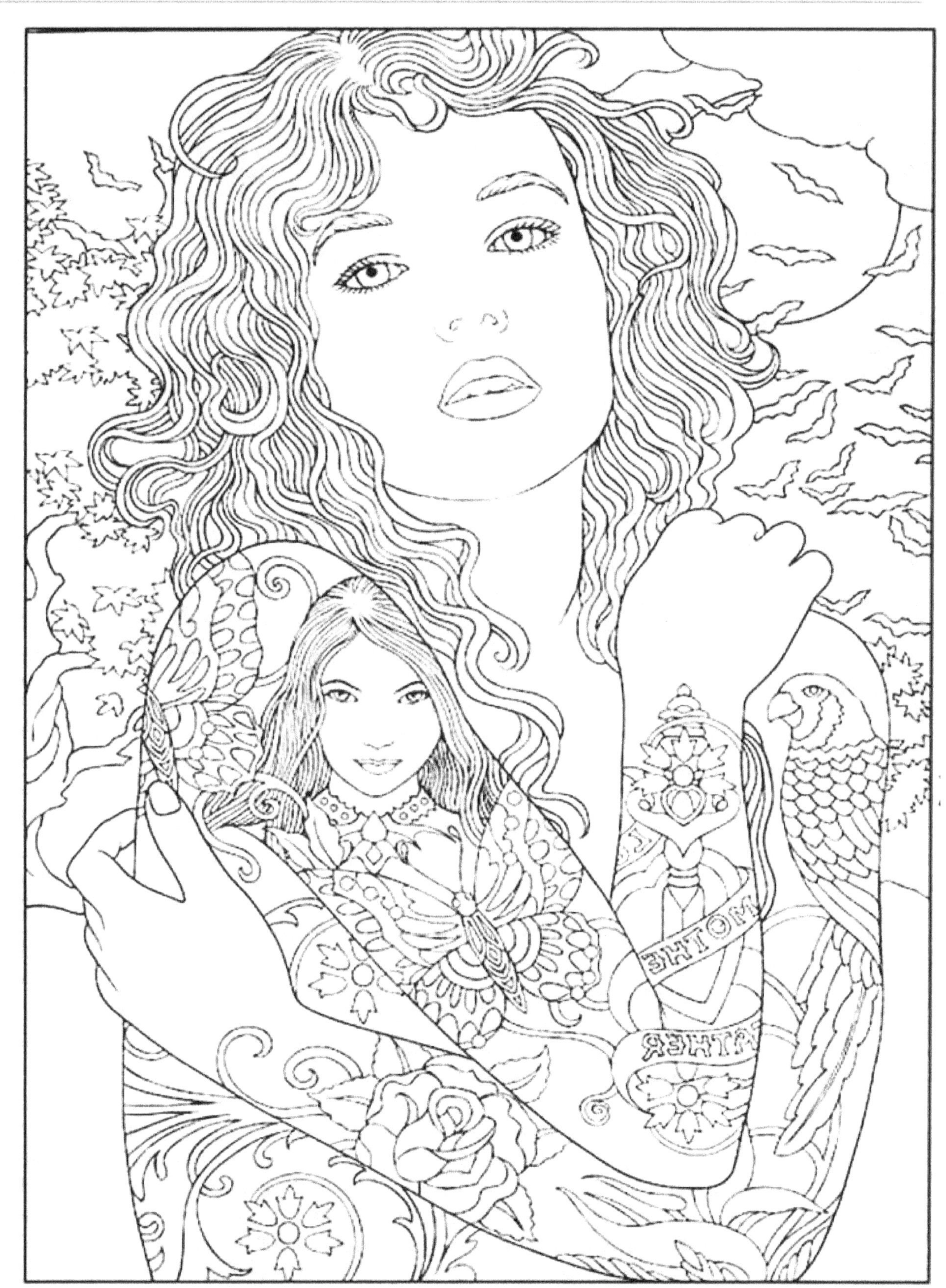

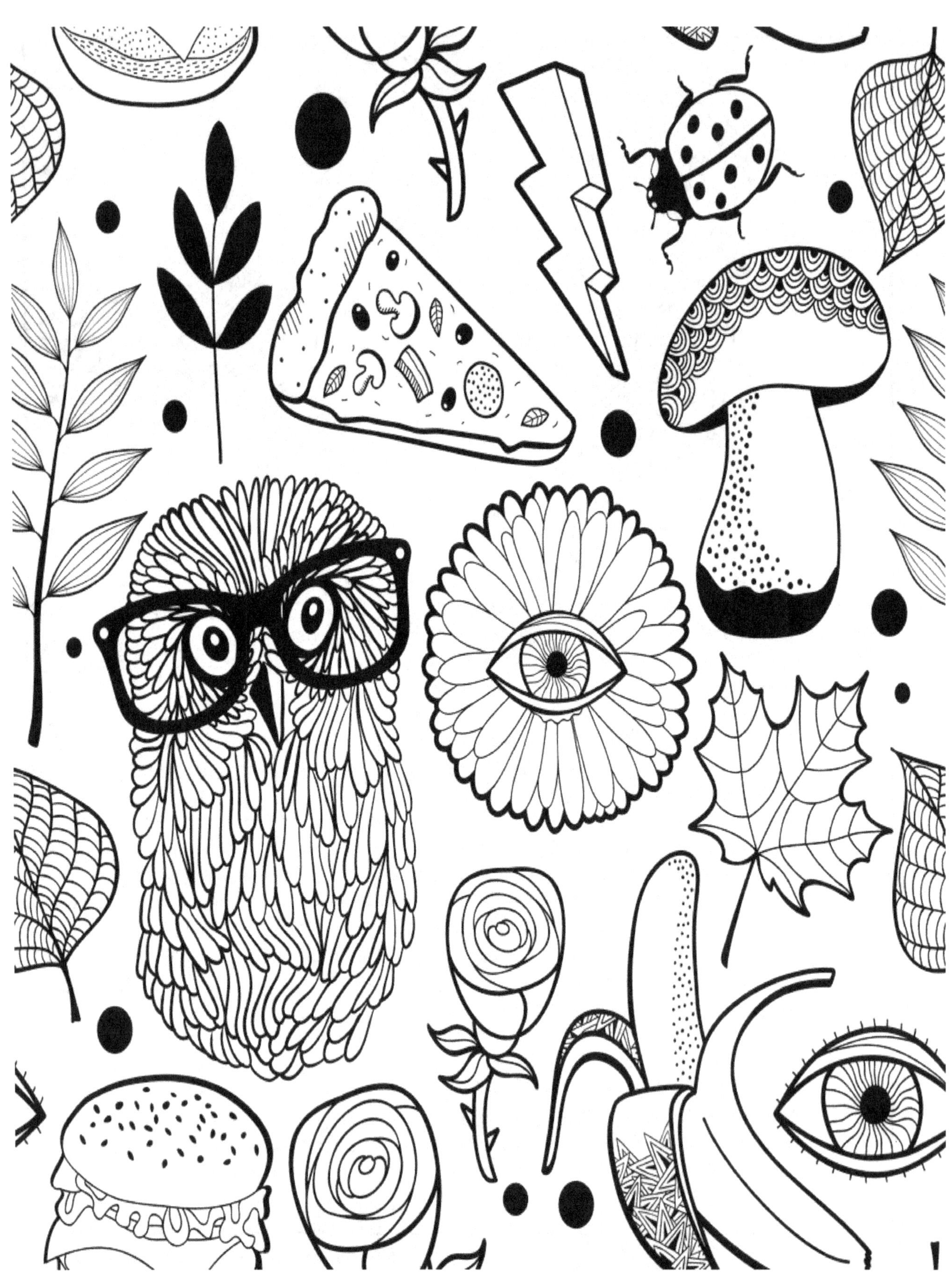

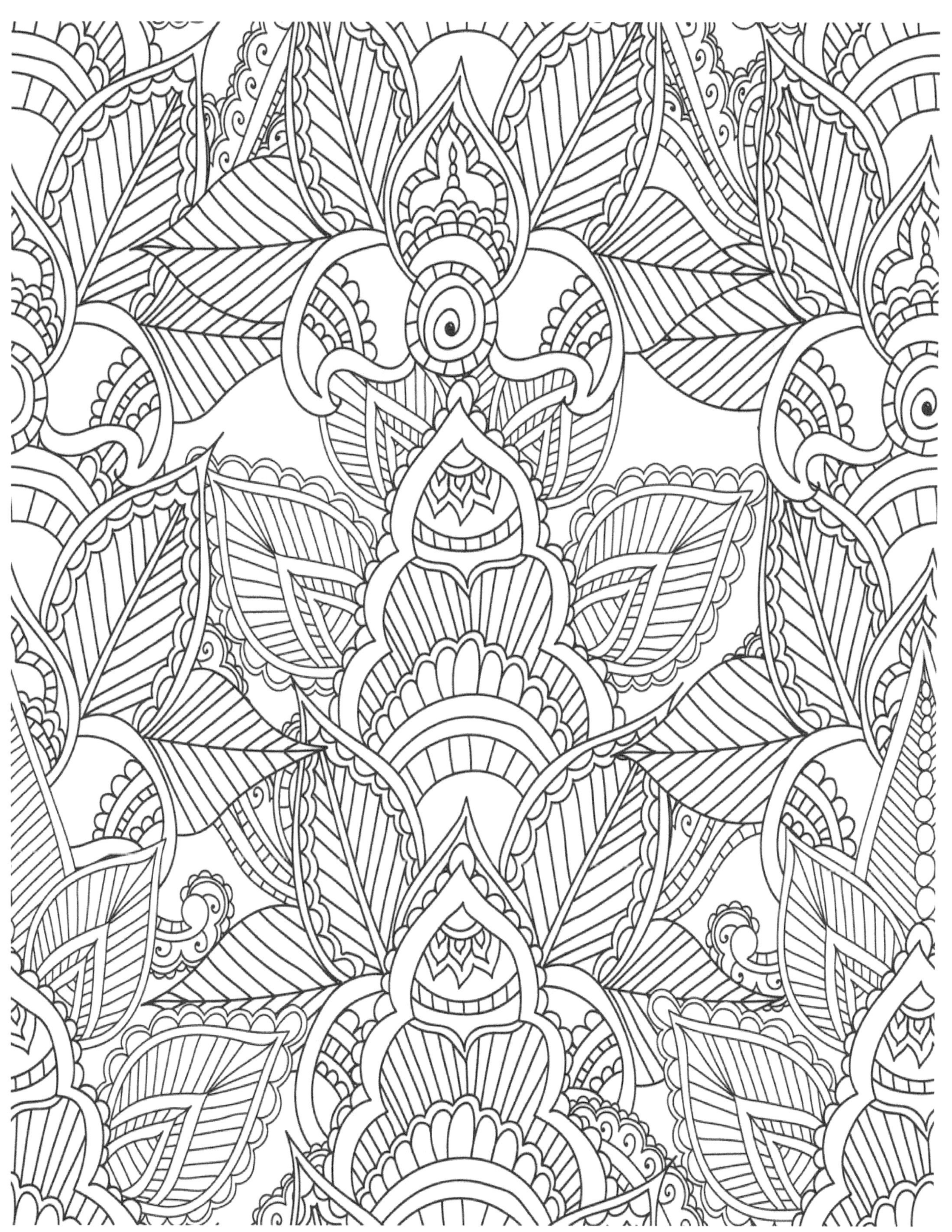

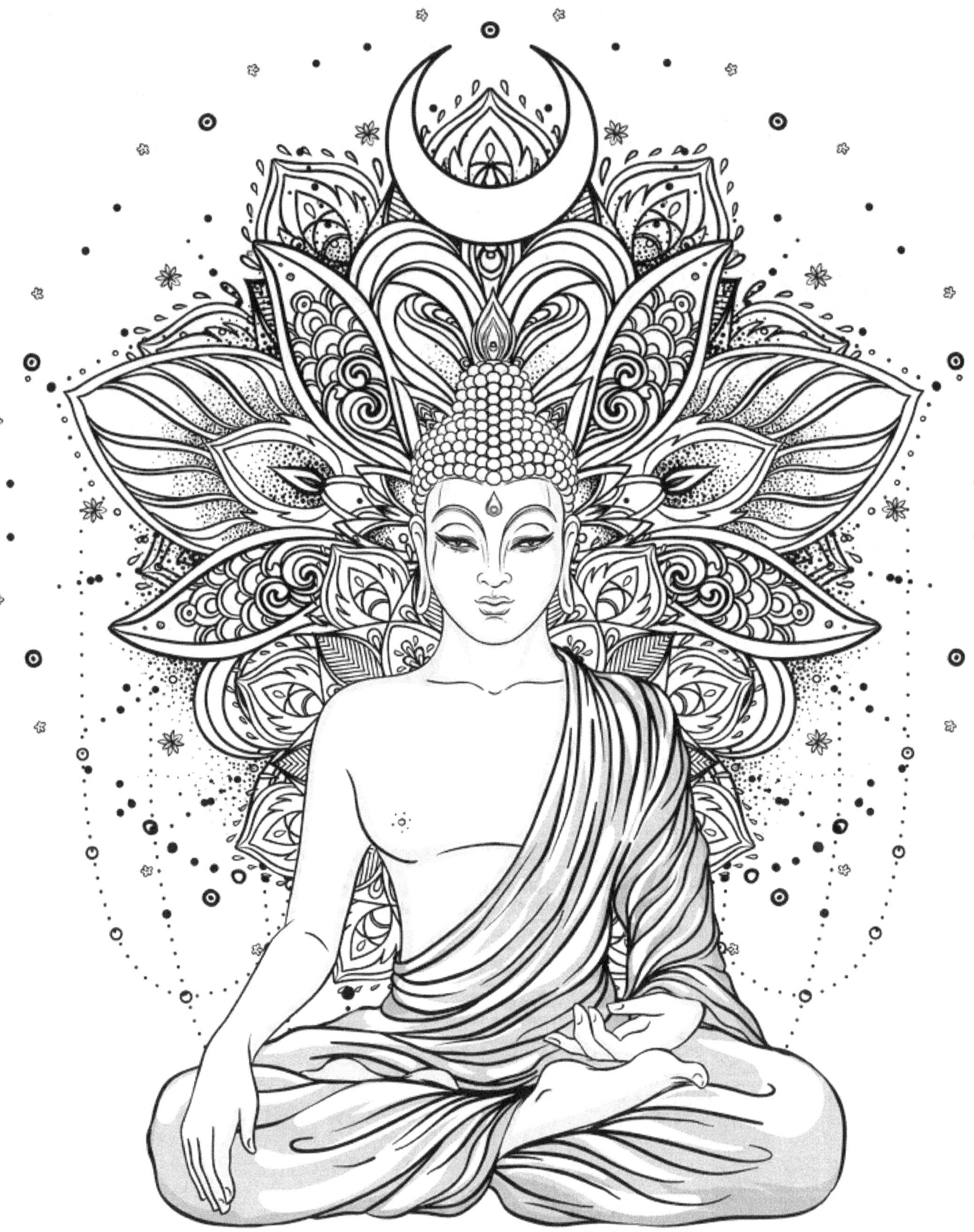

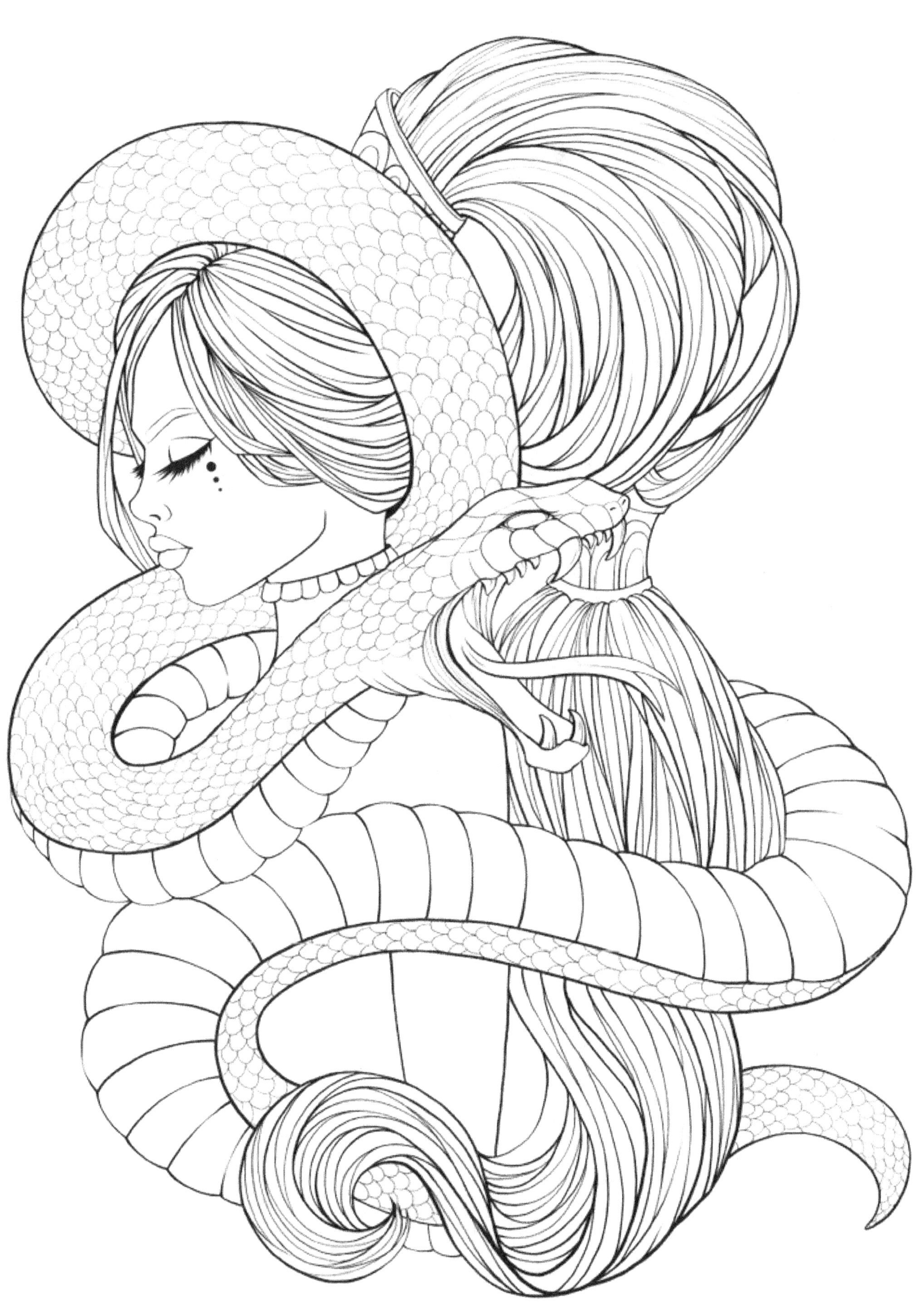

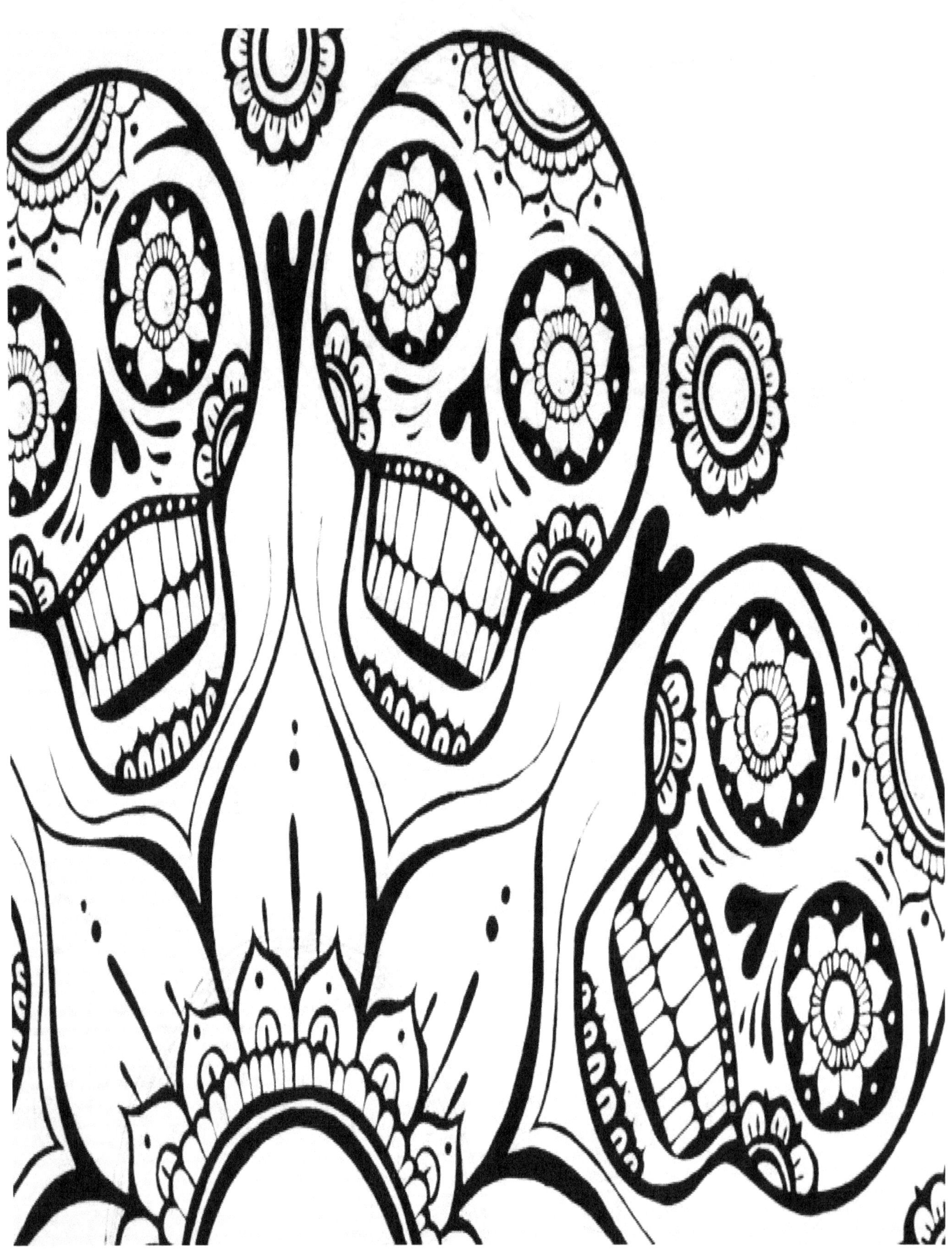

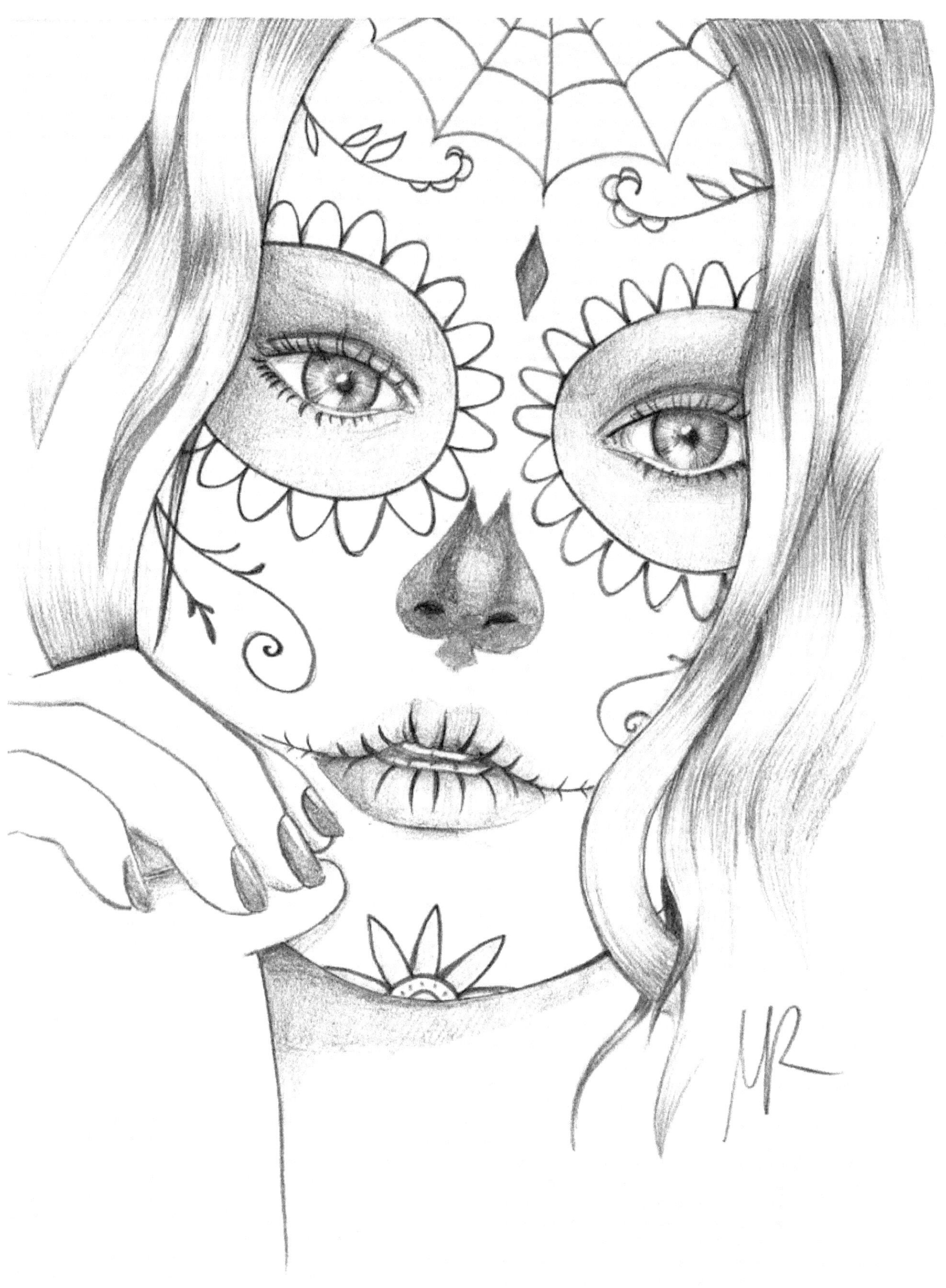

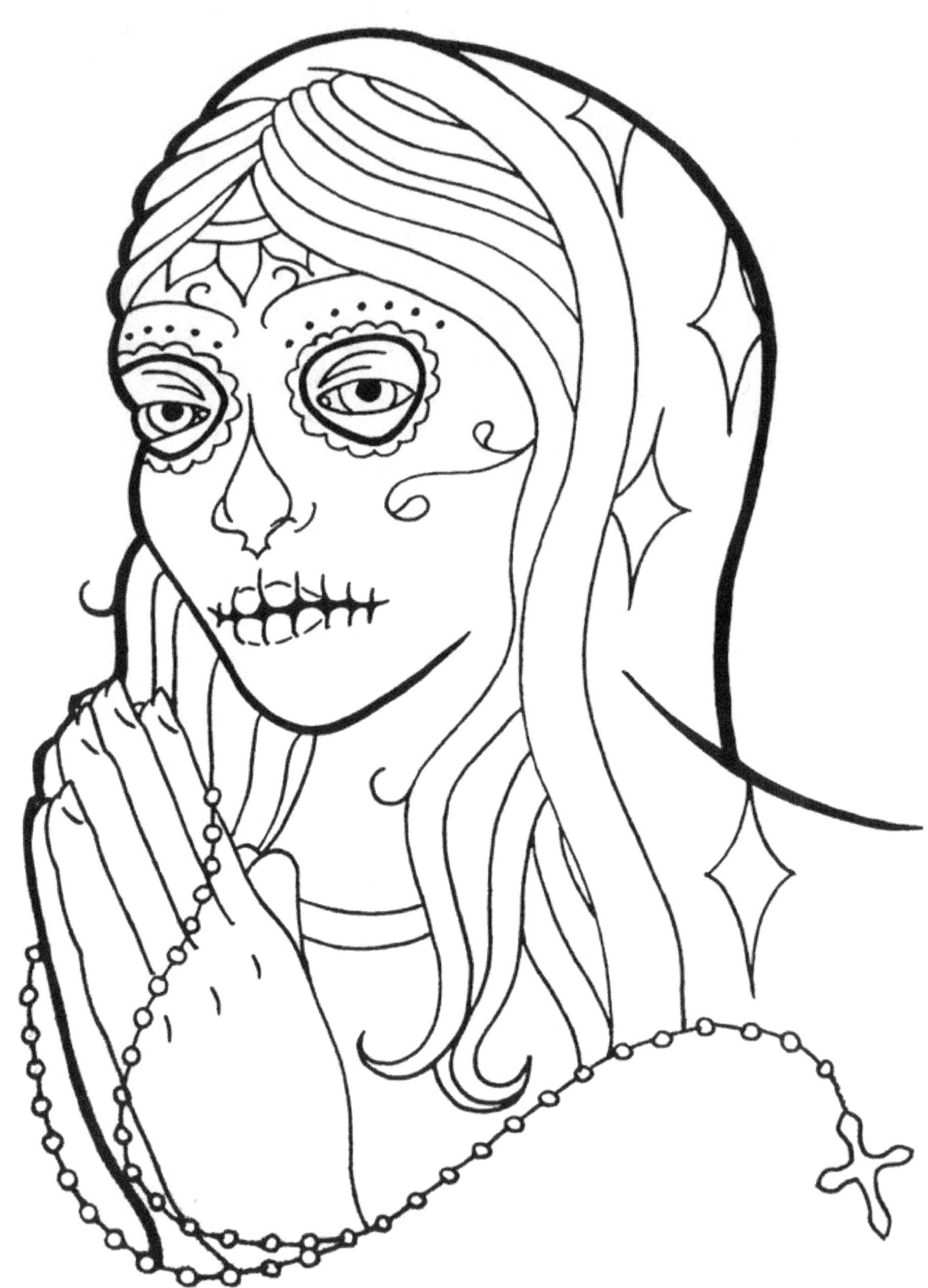

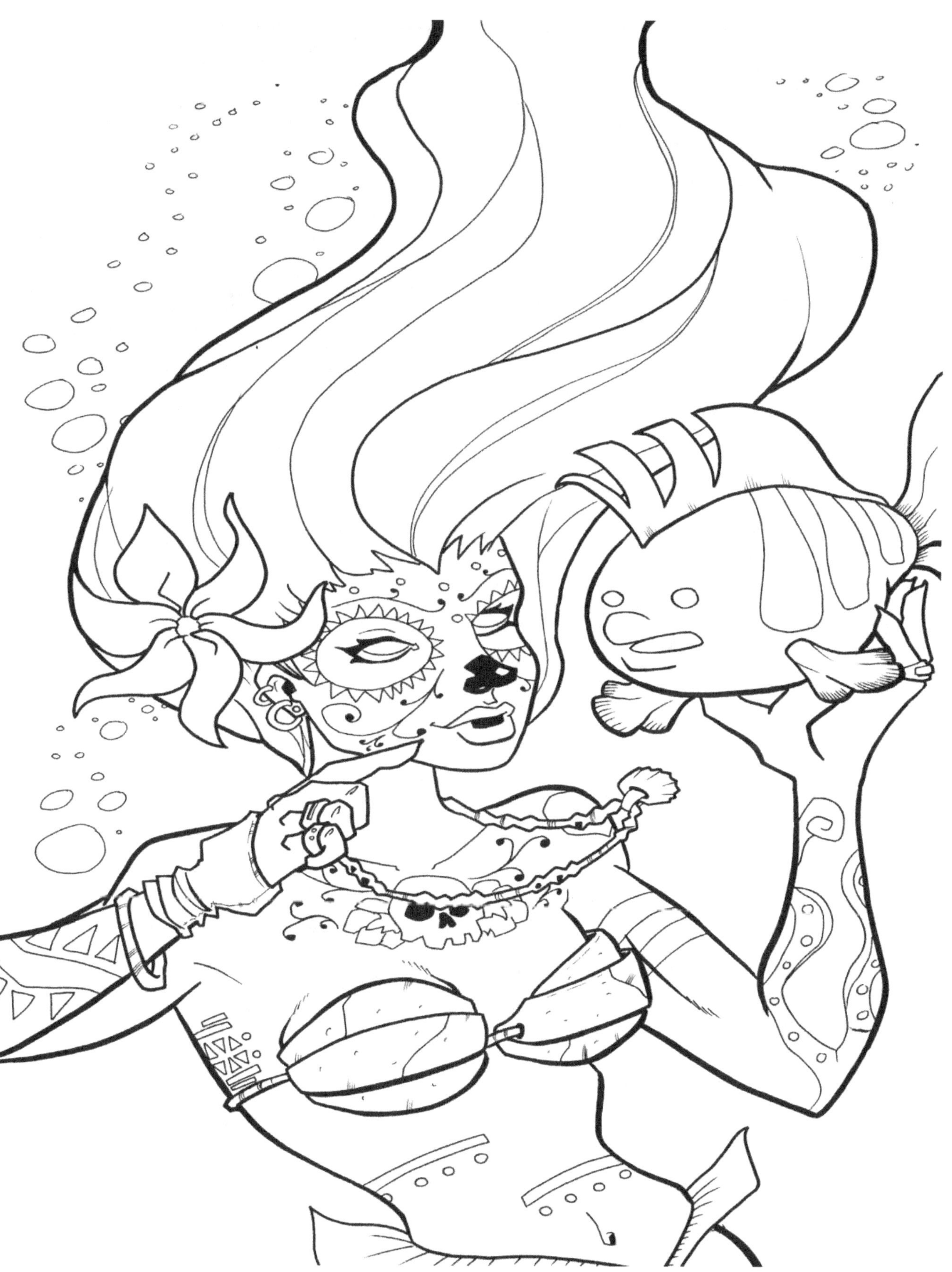

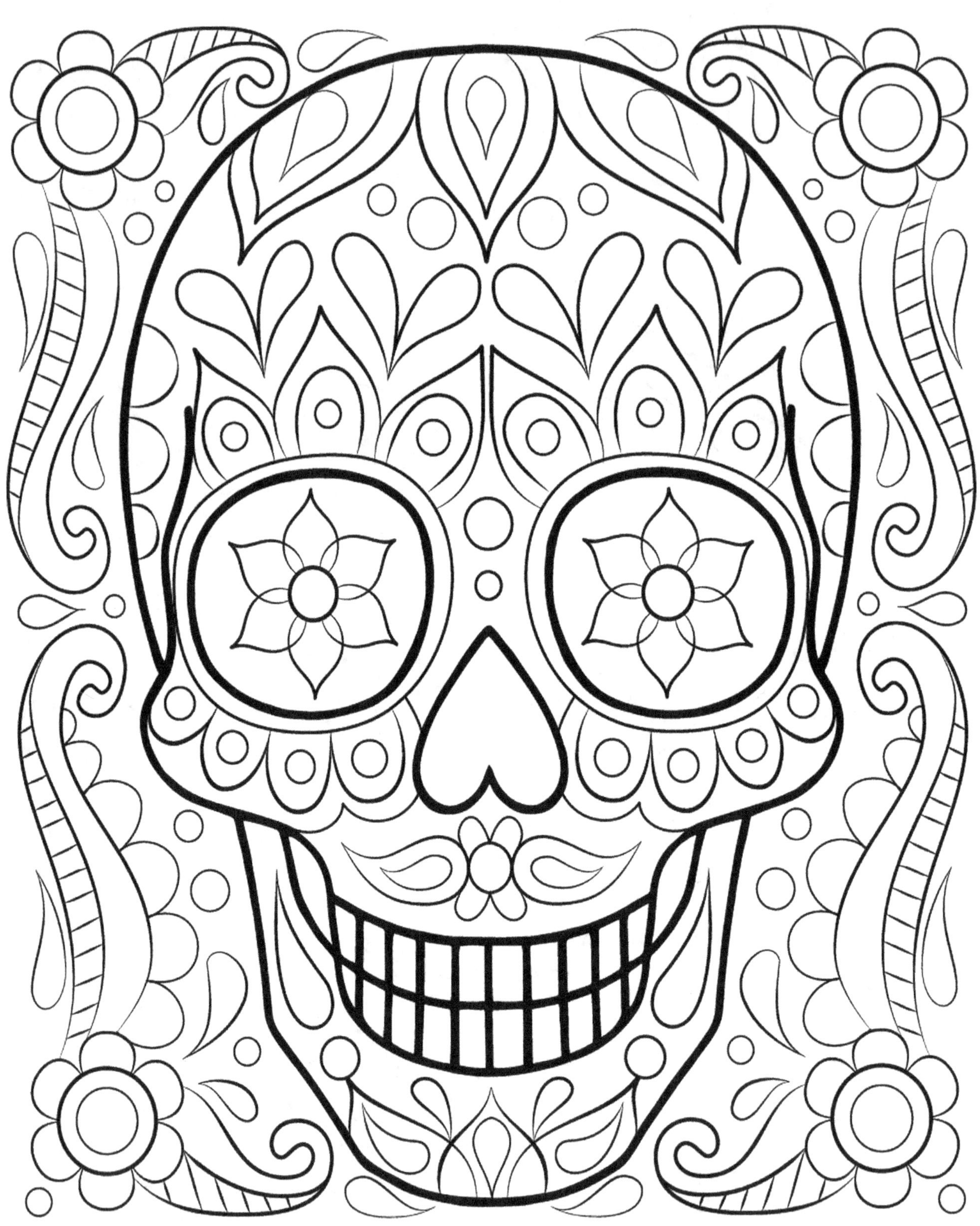